Confession

Confession

LEO TOLSTOY

Translation and Introduction by

DAVID PATTERSON

W · W · NORTON & COMPANY

NEW YORK · LONDON

Norton paperback edition reissued 1996

The text of this book is composed in photocomposition Avanta with display type set in
Centaur. Composition by Hadden Craftsmen, Inc. Manufacturing by Courier Companies, Inc.
Book design by Marjorie J. Flock.

This is a translation of *Ispoved'* as it appears in Tolstoy's *Polnoe sobranie sochinenii,*
volume 23 (Moscow, 1957), to which acknowledgment is made.

Library of Congress Cataloging in Publication Data
Tolstoy, Leo, graf, 1828–1910.
   Confession
   Translation of: Ispoved'.
   Bibliography: p.
   1. Christian life.   2. Faith.   3. Tolstoy, Leo.
graf. 1828–1910.   I. Patterson, David.   II. Title.
BV4501.T64 1983   201   83–2414

ISBN 0-393-31475-8

W. W. Norton & Company, Inc.
500 Fifth Avenue, New York, N.Y. 10110
www.wwnorton.com

W. W. Norton & Company Ltd.
Castle House, 75/76 Wells Street, London W1T 3QT

5 6 7 8 9 0

INTRODUCTION

*J*N THE FALL of 1879 the fifty-one-year-old author of *War and Peace* (1869) and *Anna Karenina* (1877) came to believe that he had accomplished nothing in life and that his life was meaningless. Either of these works would have assured him a permanent place in the annals of world literature; both testified to the depth of his genius and creativity. If artistic achievement of this magnitude cannot instill life with meaning, then where is meaning to be found? Such is the "question of life" that Tolstoy addresses in his *Confession*, a question as timeless as the spirit.

Ernest J. Simmons has described the *Confession* as "one of the noblest and most courageous utterances of man, the outpourings of a soul perplexed in the extreme by life's great problem—the relation of man to the infinite—yet executed with complete sincerity and high art."* It is a tale of midlife spiritual crisis, the ingredients of which had been fermenting in the man since his youth. As such, the *Confession* marks a turning point in Tolstoy's concern as an author, and after 1880 his attention was concentrated quite explicitly and almost exclusively on the religious life that he believed to be idealized in the peasant.

Although there are parallels between the torments of Levin in *Anna Karenina* and Tolstoy's own conflicts in the *Confession*,

---

*Ernest J. Simmons, *Leo Tolstoy* (Boston: Little, Brown and Co., 1946), p. 326.

the latter was written two years after the publication of the former and represents a more developed reflection on the question of life's meaning and the problems surrounding faith; indeed, these are precisely the difficulties that confront many of the characters in his later fiction, including the title characters in *The Death of Ivan Il'ich* (1886) and *Father Sergius* (1896), as well as Brekhunov in *Master and Man* (1895) and Nekhlyudov in *Resurrection* (1900). After completing *Anna Karenina* Tolstoy attempted to do a few idyllic sketches of peasant life, but his preoccupation with faith, death, and the meaning of life made it difficult for him to write at all.

By the end of 1877 Tolstoy was deeply entrenched in the conflict between faith and reason. During the winter of 1877–78, for example, he did some work on two pieces entitled *A Debate on Faith in the Kremlin* and *The Interlocutors* in which he set forth discussions of faith between believers and nonbelievers. He then put these projects aside to begin research for a sequel to *War and Peace* called *The Decembrists*, but his work on the new novel was interrupted for over a month in the summer of 1878 when he went on a religious retreat to Samara in southern Russia. Shortly after he returned home on 3 August he reconciled a feud with Turgenev that had lasted for seventeen years. In February of 1879, however, he ceased work on *The Decembrists* altogether and without explanation.

Tolstoy believed that one of the eternal questions for every person is the extent to which he serves God or mammon. It was with this question in mind that he began preparations for still another novel, this one entitled *One Hundred Years*. The new work was to be about Peter the Great, but by the summer of 1879 Tolstoy felt he did not have the strength to continue the project. On 14 June he went on still another religious retreat, this time to the Cave Monastery in Kiev, where he found simple monks living their lives in keeping with the "ancient Christian ways." The trip to Kiev revitalized his spirit so much that he now had the strength to break completely with the Orthodox Church, whereupon he set out to show that the teachings of the Church were not at all consistent with the Gospel. To be sure, the *Confession* was originally subtitled *An Introduction to an Unpublished Work*, that work being *An Investigation of Dogmatic Theology*, in which Tolstoy undertook one of his several attacks on the Church.

After completing a rough draft of the *Confession* at the end of 1879, Tolstoy revised it by drawing on material from his incomplete autobiographical essay, "What Am I?" The *Confession* was supposed to have appeared in 1882 in an issue of *Russkaya mysl'*, but due to difficulties with the censor it did not appear until 1884, when it was published in Geneva. It should be noted that the piece did not bear the title *Confession* until it came out in the Geneva edition.

In order to show what the censor found so objectionable about the *Confession*, it may be helpful to reproduce here the first page from the Geneva edition, which was supposed to have served as an introduction to the aborted Russian edition:

"In this work by Count L. N. Tolstoy, which we are publishing here, there unfolds before the reader the internal drama of a mighty soul in all its depth and profundity, with all its terrible and tragic turmoil. This is a soul gifted with a wealth of creative power, striving since his earliest years toward self-perfection; but he is also a soul educated in surroundings where everyone lives according to his basic origins, which not only have nothing to do with the teachings of doctrine but for the most part are in opposition to them—'wherever the teachings of doctrine exist,' formally and coldly taught, 'supported by force, those teachings are not part of the life of the people and the relations among them.'

"Here unfolds the drama of a soul who has sought from his earliest years the path to truth, or as the author refers to it, 'the meaning of life.' This is a soul striving with all the strength of his inner energy toward the light which shapes him and his edification; he strives no less by means of a scientifically cold, rational, abstract investigation that ultimately leads to God and divine truth. It is truly a magnificent drama for anyone whose living soul has the power to understand and perceive its inner meaning; it is written by the hand of one who himself lived through all its internal collisions, torments and agonies, by the hand of our ingenious writer. Under such circumstances whatever one might say about this work would seem superfluous. Nevertheless, we wish to warn the reader not to make the mistake which is so easily made by anyone who picks up a new publication, whether it deals with heartless nature or with the spirit, which is the realm of literature. The mistake stems from the manner in which the reader treats the work, the way he approaches it and the things he demands from it. Nothing of that sort should distort the author's thoughts; nothing should pervert or obscure the true meaning of his work, such as our preconceptions according to which we may view the work whenever we enter it with arbitrary questions which the author does not wish to answer and with which he did not think to concern himself."*

Finally, it may be asked whether Tolstoy ever actually found the meaning of life or the truth he sought. Whatever is said in this regard, it is clear that he continued his search until his death in 1910: his was a life characterized as much by seeking as by finding. Indeed, the meaning he was striving for reveals itself more

*Translated from N. N. Gusev, *Lev Nikolaevich Tolstoy*, vol. 3 (Moscow, 1963), p. 593.

in the search than in the discovery, and asking the question of life is more vital than answering it. For it is by raising the question that the spirit engages in its struggle for voice, a struggle that finds its expression in works such as the *Confession*.

Confession

I

*J*WAS BAPTIZED and educated in the Orthodox Christian faith. Even as a child and throughout my adolescence and youth I was schooled in the Orthodox beliefs. But when at the age of eighteen I left my second year of studies at the university,* I had lost all belief in what I had been taught.

Judging from what I can remember, I never really had a serious belief. I simply trusted in what I had been taught and in the things my elders adhered to. But even this trust was very shaky.

I remember that when I was eleven years old a high-school boy named Volodin'ka M., now long since dead, visited us one Sunday with an announcement of the latest discovery made at school. The discovery was that there is no God and that the things they were teaching us were nothing but fairy tales (this was in 1838).† I remember how this news captured the interest of my older brothers; they even let me in on their discussions. I remember that we were all very excited and that we took this news to be both quite engaging and entirely possible.

I also remember the time when my older brother Dmitri, who was then at the university, suddenly gave himself over to faith with

---

*On 12 April 1847 Tolstoy asked permission to withdraw from the University of Kazan for health reasons. Shortly afterward he returned to the Tolstoy estate at Yasnaya Polyana 130 miles from Moscow.
†On 25 May of this year Tolstoy's grandmother died. Her passing filled him with horror and left him preoccupied with death for months afterward.

all the passion that is peculiar to his nature; he began to attend all the church services, to fast, and to lead a pure and moral life. All of us, including those who were older, continually subjected him to ridicule, and for some reason we gave him the nickname of Noah. I remember that when Musin-Pushkin, then a trustee of the University of Kazan, invited us to a ball, my brother declined the invitation; Musin-Pushkin, with a certain mockery, tried to persuade him to come by saying that even David danced before the ark. At that time I sympathized with these jokes from my elders, and they led me to the conclusion that I had to learn my catechism and go to church but that it was not necessary to take it all too seriously. I also remember reading Voltaire* when I was very young; not only was I not disgusted with his mockery, but I actually found it quite amusing.

My break with faith occurred in me as it did and still does among people of our social and cultural type. As I see it, in most cases it happens like this: people live as everyone lives, but they all live according to principles that not only have nothing to do with the teachings of faith but for the most part are contrary to them. The teachings of faith have no place in life and never come into play in the relations among people; they simply play no role in living life itself. The teachings of faith are left to some other realm, separated from life and independent of it. If one should encounter them, then it is only as some superficial phenomenon that has no connection with life.

Today, as in days past, there is no way to tell from a person's life, from his deeds, whether or not he is a believer. If there is

*François Marie Arouet de Voltaire (1694–1778) was a French philosopher, dramatist, essayist, poet, historian, and satirist. A center of controversy throughout his life, he became the spokesman for the anticlerical and rationalist ideas of the Age of Enlightenment.

indeed no difference between those who are clearly adherents of the Orthodox faith and those who deny it, then it is not to the benefit of the former. Then, as now, the open avowal and confession of the Orthodox faith occurred largely among narrow-minded, cruel, and immoral people wrapped up in their own self-importance. On the other hand, intellect, honor, straightforwardness, good naturedness, and morality were for the most part to be found among people claiming to be disbelievers.

They teach catechism in the schools and send pupils to church; functionaries must carry certificates showing they have taken holy communion. But now, and even more so in the past, a person of our class who is no longer in school and has not gone into public service can live dozens of years without once being reminded that he lives among Christians, while he himself is regarded as a follower of the Orthodox Christian faith.

Thus today, as in days past, the teachings of faith, accepted on trust and sustained by external pressure, gradually fade under the influence of the knowledge and experiences of life, which stand in opposition to those teachings. Quite often a man goes on for years imagining that the religious teaching that had been imparted to him since childhood is still intact, while all the time there is not a trace of it left in him.

A certain intelligent and honest man named S. once told me the story of how he ceased to be a believer. At the age of twenty-six, while taking shelter for the night during a hunting trip, he knelt to pray in the evening, as had been his custom since childhood. His older brother, who had accompanied him on the trip, was lying down on some straw and watching him. When S. had finished and was getting ready to lie down, his brother said to him, "So you still do that." And they said nothing more to each other. From that day S. gave up praying and going to church. And for thirty years he has not prayed, he has not taken holy communion, and he has not gone to church. Not because he shared his brother's convictions and went along with them; nor was it because he had decided on something or other in his own soul. It was simply that the remark his brother had made was like the nudge of a finger against a wall that was about to fall over from its own weight. His brother's remark showed him that the place where he thought faith to be had long since been empty; subsequently the words he spoke, the signs of the cross he made, and the bowing of his head in prayer were in essence completely meaningless actions. Once having admitted the meaninglessness of these gestures, he could no longer continue them.

Thus it has happened and continues to happen, I believe, with the great majority of people. I am referring to people of our social and cultural type, people who are honest with themselves, and not those who use faith as a means of obtaining some temporal goal or other. (These people are the most radical disbelievers, for if faith, in their view, is a means of obtaining some worldly end, then it is indeed no faith at all.) People of our type are in a position where the light of knowledge and of life has broken down the artificial structure, and they have either taken note of this and have left it behind them or they have remained unconscious of it.

The teachings of faith instilled in me since childhood left me, just as they have left others; the only difference is that since I began reading and thinking a great deal at an early age, I became aware of my renunciation of the teachings of faith very early in life. From the age of sixteen I gave up praying and on my own accord quit going to church and fasting. I ceased to believe in what had been instilled in me since childhood, yet I did believe in something, though I could not say what. I even believed in God —or rather I did not deny God—but what kind of God I could not say; nor did I deny Christ and his teachings, but I could not have said what those teachings consisted of.

As I now look back at that time I clearly see that apart from animal instincts, the faith that affected my life, the only real faith I had, was faith in perfection. But I could not have said what perfection consisted of or what its purpose might be. I tried to achieve intellectual perfection; I studied everything I could, everything that life gave me a chance to study. I tried to perfect my will and set up rules for myself that I endeavored to follow. I strove for physical perfection by doing all the exercises that develop strength and agility and by undergoing all the hardships that discipline the self in endurance and perseverance. I took all this to be perfection. The starting point of it all was, of course, moral perfection, but this was soon replaced by a belief in overall perfection, that is, a desire to be better not in my own eyes or in the eyes of God, but rather a desire to be better in the eyes of other people. And this effort to be better in the eyes of other people was very quickly displaced by a longing to be stronger than other people, that is, more renowned, more important, wealthier than others.

II

Someday I shall relate the story of my life, including both the pathetic and the instructive aspects of those ten years of my youth. I think that many, very many, have had the same experiences. With all my soul I longed to be good; but I was young, I had passions, and I was alone, utterly alone, whenever I sought what was good. Every time I tried to express my most heartfelt desires to be morally good I met with contempt and ridicule; and as soon as I would give in to vile passions I was praised and encouraged. Ambition, love of power, self-interest, lechery, pride, anger, vengeance—all of it was highly esteemed. As I gave myself over to these passions I became like my elders, and I felt that they were pleased with me. A kindhearted aunt of mine with whom I lived, one of the finest of women, was forever telling me that her fondest desire was for me to have an affair with a married woman: *"Rien ne forme un jeune homme comme une liaison avec une femme comme il faut."** Another happiness she wished for me was that I become an adjutant, preferably to the emperor. And the greatest happiness of all would be for me to marry a very wealthy young lady who could bring me as many serfs as possible.

I cannot recall those years without horror, loathing, and heart-rending pain. I killed people in war, challenged men to duels with the purpose of killing them, and lost at cards; I squandered the fruits of the peasants' toil and then had them executed; I was a fornicator and a cheat. Lying, stealing, promiscuity of every kind, drunkenness, violence, murder—there was not a crime I did not commit; yet in spite of it all I was praised, and my colleagues considered me and still do consider me a relatively moral man.

Thus I lived for ten years.

During this time I began to write out of vanity, self-interest, and pride. I did the same thing in my writing that I did in my life. In order to acquire the fame and the money I was writing for, it was necessary to conceal what was good and to flaunt what was bad. And that is what I did. Time after time I would scheme in my writings to conceal under the mask of indifference and even pleasantry those yearnings for something good which gave meaning to my life. And I succeeded in this and was praised.

At the age of twenty-six, when the war had ended,† I came to St. Petersburg and got to know the writers there. They accepted me as one of their own, heaped flattery upon me. Before I could

---

*"Nothing shapes a young man like a liaison with a decent woman."
†This was the Crimean War (1853–56), in which England, France, Turkey, and Sardinia combined forces to defeat Russia.

turn around, the views on life peculiar to the writers with whom I associated became my own, and before long all my previous efforts to become better were completely at an end. Having no discipline myself, I let these views justify my life.

The theory adopted by these people, my fellow writers, was that life proceeds according to a general development and that we, the thinkers, play the primary role in that development; moreover, we, the artists and the poets, have the greatest influence on the thinkers. Our mission is to educate people. In order to avoid the obvious question—"What do I know and what can I teach?"—the theory explained that it is not necessary to know anything and that the artist and the poet teach unconsciously. Since I was considered a remarkable artist and poet, it was quite natural for me to embrace this theory. As an artist and poet I wrote and taught without myself knowing what I was teaching. I received money for doing this; I enjoyed excellent food, lodgings, women, society; I was famous. Therefore whatever I was teaching must have been very good.

This faith in knowledge, poetry, and the evolution of life was indeed a faith, and I was one of its priests. Being one of its priests was very profitable and quite pleasant. I lived a rather long time in this faith without ever doubting its truth. But in the second and especially in the third year of such a way of life I began to doubt the infallibility of this faith and started to examine it more closely. The first thing that led me to doubt was that I began to notice that the priests of this faith did not agree among themselves. Some would say, "We are the best and the most useful of teachers, for we teach what is needful while others who teach are in error." Others would say, "No, we are the true teachers; it is you who are in error." They argued and quarreled among themselves and abused, deceived, and cheated one another. Moreover, there were many among us who were not even concerned about who was right and who was wrong; they simply pursued their own selfish ends and had the support of our activity. All this forced me to doubt the truth of our faith.

Furthermore, once I had come to doubt the faith of the writers, I began to observe its priests more closely and became convinced that nearly all the priests of this faith were immoral men, in most cases of a base and worthless character. Many of them were lower than those whom I had met earlier during my wanton military life, but they were complacent and self-satisfied to a degree that can only be found either among people who are complete saints or among those who do not know what holiness is. People became repugnant to me, and I became repugnant to myself. And I realized that this faith was a delusion.

But the strange thing is that even though I was quick to see the utter lie of this faith and renounced it, I did not renounce the rank bestowed upon me by these people, the rank of artist, poet, and teacher. I naïvely imagined that I was a poet and an artist, that I could teach all men without myself knowing what I was teaching. And so I went on.

As a result of my association with these people, I took up a new vice: I developed a pathological pride and the insane conviction that it was my mission to teach people without knowing what I was teaching them.

As I now look back at that period and recall my state of mind and the state of mind of those people (a state that, by the way, persists among thousands), it all seems pitiful, horrible, and ridiculous to me; it excites the same feelings one might experience in a madhouse.

At the time we were all convinced that we had to speak, write, and publish as quickly as possible and as much as possible and that this was necessary for the good of mankind. Thousands of us published and wrote in an effort to teach others, all the while disclaiming and abusing one another. Without taking note of the fact that we knew nothing, that we did not know the answer to the simplest question of life, the question of what is right and what is wrong, we all went on talking without listening to one another. At times we would indulge and praise each other on the condition that we be indulged and praised in return; at other times we would irritate and shout at each other exactly as in a madhouse.

Thousands of workers toiled day and night, to the limit of their strength, gathering and printing millions of words to be distributed by mail throughout all Russia. We continued to teach, teach, and teach some more, and there was no way we could ever teach it all; and then we would get angry because people paid us little heed.

Very strange indeed, but now I understand it. The real reason behind what we were doing was that we wanted to obtain as much money and praise as possible. Writing books and newspapers was the only thing we knew how to do in order to attain this end. And so that is what we did. But in order for us to engage in something so useless and at the same time maintain the conviction that we were very important people, we needed a rationale that would justify what we were doing. And so we came up with the following: everything that exists is rational. Further, everything that exists is evolving. And it is evolving by means of an enlightenment. The enlightenment in turn undergoes change through the distribution of books and periodicals. We are paid and respected for writing books and periodicals, and therefore we are the most useful and the best of people. This reasoning would have worked very well, had we all been in agreement; but since for every opinion expressed by one person there was always someone else whose opinion was diametrically opposed to it, we should have been led to reconsider. But we never noticed this. We received money, and people of our circle praised us; thus every one of us believed himself to be right.

It is now clear to me that there was no difference between ourselves and people living in a madhouse; at the time I only vaguely suspected this, and, like all madmen, I thought everyone except myself was mad.

III

Thus I lived, giving myself over to this insanity for another six years, until my marriage.* During this time I went abroad. Life in Europe and my acquaintance with eminent and learned Europeans confirmed me all the more in my belief in general perfectibility, for I found the very same belief among them. My belief assumed a form that it commonly assumes among the educated people of our time. This belief was expressed by the word "progress." At the time it seemed to me that this word had meaning. Like any living individual, I was tormented by questions of how to live better. I still had not understood that in answering that one must live according to progress, I was talking just like a person being carried along in a boat by the waves and the wind; without really answering, such a person replies to the only important question—"Where are we to steer?"—by saying, "We are being carried somewhere."

I did not notice this at the time. Only now and then would my feelings, and not my reason, revolt against this commonly held superstition of the age, by means of which people hide from themselves their own ignorance of life. Thus during my stay in

*On 23 September 1862, at the age of thirty-four, Tolstoy married eighteen-year-old Sof'ya Andreevna Bers.

Paris the sight of an execution revealed to me the feebleness of my superstitious belief in progress.* When I saw how the head was severed from the body and heard the thud of each part as it fell into the box, I understood, not with my intellect but with my whole being, that no theories of the rationality of existence or of progress could justify such an act; I realized that even if all the people in the world from the day of creation found this to be necessary according to whatever theory, I knew that it was not necessary and that it was wrong. Therefore, my judgments must be based on what is right and necessary and not on what people say and do; I must judge not according to progress but according to my own heart. The death of my brother was another instance in which I realized the inadequacy of the superstition of progress in regard to life.† A good, intelligent, serious man, he was still young when he fell ill. He suffered for over a year and died an agonizing death without ever understanding why he lived and understanding even less why he was dying. No theories could provide any answers to these questions, either for him or for me, during his slow and painful death.

But these were only rare instances of doubt; on the whole I continued to live, embracing only a faith in progress. "Everything is developing, and I am developing; the reason why I am developing in this way will come to light, along with everything else." Thus I was led to formulate my faith at the time.

When I returned from abroad I settled in the country and

*On 25 March 1857 François Riche was executed for murder. On 6 April Tolstoy mentioned the execution in his diary: "He kissed the Gospel and then—death. What insanity!"
†Tolstoy's favorite brother, Nikolai, died of consumption on 20 September 1860 at the age of thirty-seven. On 21 January 1856 his brother Dmitri died of the same disease at the age of twenty-eight. Although Dmitri served as a model for Levin's brother in *Anna Karenina* (1877), here Tolstoy is probably referring to the death of Nikolai.

occupied myself with the peasant schools. This occupation was especially dear to my heart because it involved none of the lies that had become so apparent to me, the lies that had irritated me when I was a literary teacher. Here too I was acting in the name of progress, but I assumed a critical attitude toward that progress. I told myself that in many of its forms progress did not proceed as it should and that here it was necessary to leave a primitive people, the peasant children, completely free to choose the path of progress they wanted.

In essence I was still faced with the same insoluble problem of how to teach without knowing what I was teaching. In the higher spheres of literature it was clear to me that I could not teach without knowing what I was teaching; for I saw that everyone taught differently and that in the arguments they had they scarcely hid their ignorance from each other. But here, with the peasant children, I thought I could get around this difficulty by allowing the children to learn whatever they liked. It now seems ludicrous to me when I recall how I tried this and that in order to carry out this whim of mine to teach, all the while knowing full well in the depths of my soul that there was no way I could teach what was needful because I did not know what was needful. After a year of being occupied with school I went abroad once again in order to find out how this could be done without myself knowing how to teach.

I believed that I had found a solution abroad, and, armed with all this wisdom, I returned to Russia in the year of the emancipation of the serfs.* I took up the office of arbitrator and began teaching the uneducated people in the schools and the educated people through the periodical that I had started publishing. Things seemed to be going well, but I felt that my mental health

*On 18 February 1861 Tsar Alexander II published his imperial manifesto abolishing serfdom.

was not what it should be and that this could not go on for long. Perhaps even then I would have fallen into the despair that came over me at the age of fifty were it not for one more aspect of life which I had not yet experienced and which held the promise of salvation: family life.

For a year I was occupied with arbitration, with the schools, and with the magazine. But I was soon exhausted from being entangled in the whole thing. The struggle with arbitration became burdensome to me; my activity in the schools was a lot of trouble; and my shuffling around with the magazine became repugnant to me, since it was forever centered on the same thing —the desire to teach everyone while hiding the fact that I did not know what I was teaching. It finally reached a point where I fell ill, more spiritually than physically; I gave it all up and went to the steppes of the Bashkirs to breathe fresh air, drink *koumiss*, and live an animal life.

After I returned I got married. The new circumstances of a happy family life completely diverted me from any search for the overall meaning of life. At that time my whole life was focused on my family, my wife, my children, and thus on a concern for improving our way of life. My striving for personal perfection, which had already been replaced by a striving for perfection in general, a striving for progress, now became a striving for what was best for my family and me.

Thus another fifteen years went by.

In spite of the fact that during these fifteen years I regarded writing as a trivial endeavor, I continued to write.* I had already tasted the temptations of authorship, the temptations of enormous monetary rewards and applause for worthless work, and I gave myself up to it as a means of improving my material situation

*It was during this period, when he "regarded writing as a trivial endeavor," that Tolstoy produced *War and Peace* (1869).

and as a way of stifling any questions in my soul concerning the meaning of my life and of life in general.

As I wrote I taught what to me was the only truth: that we must live for whatever is best for ourselves and our family.

And so I lived. But five years ago something very strange began to happen to me. At first I began having moments of bewilderment, when my life would come to a halt, as if I did not know how to live or what to do; I would lose my presence of mind and fall into a state of depression. But this passed, and I continued to live as before. Then the moments of bewilderment recurred more frequently, and they always took the same form. Whenever my life came to a halt, the questions would arise: Why? And what next?

At first I thought these were pointless and irrelevent questions. I thought that the answers to them were well known and that if I should ever want to resolve them, it would not be too hard for me; it was just that I could not be bothered with it now, but if I should take it upon myself, then I would find the answers. But the questions began to come up more and more frequently, and their demands to be answered became more and more urgent. And like points concentrated into one spot, these questions without answers came together to form a single black stain.

It happened with me as it happens with everyone who contracts a fatal internal disease. At first there were the insignificant symptoms of an ailment, which the patient ignores; then these symptoms recur more and more frequently, until they merge into one continuous duration of suffering. The suffering increases, and before he can turn around the patient discovers what he already knew: the thing he had taken for a mere indisposition is in fact the most important thing on earth to him, is in fact death.

This is exactly what happened to me. I realized that this was not an incidental ailment but something very serious, and that if the same questions should continue to recur, I would have to answer them. And I tried to answer them. The questions seemed to be such foolish, simple, childish questions. But as soon as I laid my hands on them and tried to resolve them, I was immediately convinced, first of all, that they were not childish and foolish questions but the most vital and profound questions in life, and, secondly, that no matter how much I pondered them there was no way I could resolve them. Before I could be occupied with my Samara estate, with the education of my son, or with the writing of books, I had to know why I was doing these things. As long as I do not know the reason why, I cannot do anything. In the middle of my concern with the household, which at the time kept me quite busy, a question would suddenly come into my head: "Very well, you will have 6,000 desyatins* in the Samara province, as well as 300 horses; what then?" And I was completely taken aback and did not know what else to think. As soon as I started to think about the education of my children, I would ask myself, "Why?" Or I would reflect on how the people might attain prosperity, and I would suddenly ask myself, "What concern is it of mine?" Or in the middle of thinking about the fame that my works were bringing me I would say to myself, "Very well, you will be more famous than Gogol, Pushkin, Shakespeare, Molière, more famous than all the writers in the world—so what?

And I could find absolutely no reply.

IV

My life came to a stop. I could breathe, eat, drink, and sleep; indeed, I could not help but breathe, eat, drink, and sleep. But there was no life in me because I had no desires whose satisfaction

*One desyatin is equal to 2.7 acres, giving Tolstoy 16,200 acres in the Samsara province.

I would have found reasonable. If I wanted something, I knew beforehand that it did not matter whether or not I got it.

If a fairy had come and offered to fulfill my every wish, I would not have known what to wish for. If in moments of intoxication I should have not desires but the habits of old desires, in moments of sobriety I knew that it was all a delusion, that I really desired nothing. I did not even want to discover truth anymore because I had guessed what it was. The truth was that life is meaningless.

It was as though I had lived a little, wandered a little, until I came to the precipice, and I clearly saw that there was nothing ahead except ruin. And there was no stopping, no turning back, no closing my eyes so I would not see that there was nothing ahead except the deception of life and of happiness and the reality of suffering and death, of complete annihilation.

I grew sick of life; some irresistible force was leading me to somehow get rid of it. It was not that I wanted to kill myself. The force that was leading me away from life was more powerful, more absolute, more all-encompassing than any desire. With all my strength I struggled to get away from life. The thought of suicide came to me as naturally then as the thought of improving life had come to me before. This thought was such a temptation that I had to use cunning against myself in order not to go through with it too hastily. I did not want to be in a hurry only because I wanted to use all my strength to untangle my thoughts. If I could not get them untangled, I told myself, I could always go ahead with it. And there I was, a fortunate man, carrying a rope from my room, where I was alone every night as I undressed, so that I would not hang myself from the beam between the closets. And I quit going hunting with a gun, so that I would not be too easily tempted to rid myself of life. I myself did not know what I wanted. I was afraid of life, I struggled to get rid of it, and yet I hoped for something from it.

And this was happening to me at a time when, from all indications, I should have been considered a completely happy man; this was when I was not yet fifty years old. I had a good, loving, and beloved wife, fine children, and a large estate that was growing and expanding without any effort on my part. More than ever before I was respected by friends and acquaintances, praised by strangers, and I could claim a certain renown without really deluding myself. Moreover, I was not physically and mentally unhealthy; on the contrary, I enjoyed a physical and mental vigor such as I had rarely encountered among others my age. Physically, I could keep up with the peasants working in the fields; mentally, I could work eight and ten hours at a stretch without suffering any aftereffects from the strain. And in such a state of affairs I came to a point where I could not live; and even though I feared death, I had to employ ruses against myself to keep from committing suicide.

I described my spiritual condition to myself in this way: my life is some kind of stupid and evil practical joke that someone is playing on me. In spite of the fact that I did not acknowledge the existence of any "Someone" who might have created me, the notion that someone brought me into the world as a stupid and evil joke seemed to be the most natural way to describe my condition.

I could not help imagining that somewhere there was someone who was now amusing himself, laughing at me and at the way I had lived for thirty or forty years, studying, developing, growing in body and soul; laughing at how I had now completely matured intellectually and had reached that summit from which life reveals itself only to stand there like an utter fool, clearly seeing that there is nothing in life, that there never was and never will be. "And it makes him laugh . . ."

But whether or not there actually was someone laughing at me did not make it any easier for me. I could not attach a rational ◄— meaning to a single act in my entire life. The only thing that amazed me was how I had failed to realize this in the very beginning. All this had been common knowledge for so long. If not today, then tomorrow sickness and death will come (indeed, they were already approaching) to everyone, to me, and nothing will remain except the stench and the worms. My deeds, whatever they may be, will be forgotten sooner or later, and I myself will be no more. Why, then, do anything? How can anyone fail to see this and live? That's what is amazing! It is possible to live only as long as life intoxicates us; once we are sober we cannot help seeing that it is all a delusion, a stupid delusion! Nor is there anything funny or witty about it; it is only cruel and stupid.

There is an old Eastern fable about a traveler who was taken by surprise in the steppes by a raging wild beast. Trying to save himself from the beast, the traveler jumps into a dried-up well; but at the bottom of the well he sees a dragon with its jaws open wide, waiting to devour him. The unhappy man does not dare climb out for fear of being killed by the wild beast, and he does not dare jump to the bottom of the well for fear of being devoured by the dragon. So he grabs hold of a branch of a wild bush growing in the crevices of the well and clings to it. His arms grow weak, and he feels that soon he must fall prey to the death that awaits him on either side. Yet he still holds on, and while he is clinging to the branch he looks up to see two mice, one black and one white, evenly working their way around the branch of the bush he is hanging from, gnawing on it. Soon the bush will give way and break off, and he will fall into the jaws of the dragon. The traveler sees this and knows that he will surely die. But while he is still hanging there he looks around and sees some drops of honey on the leaves of the bush, and he stretches out his tongue and licks them. Thus I cling to the branch of life, knowing that inevitably the dragon of death is waiting, ready to tear me to pieces; and I cannot understand why this torment has befallen me. I try to suck the honey that once consoled me, but the honey is no longer sweet. Day and night the black mouse and the white mouse gnaw at the branch to which I cling. I clearly see the dragon, and the honey has lost all its sweetness. I see only the inescapable dragon and the mice, and I cannot turn my eyes from them. This is no fairy tale but truth, irrefutable and understood by all.

The former delusion of the happiness of life that had concealed from me the horror of the dragon no longer deceives me. No matter how much I tell myself that I cannot understand the meaning of life, that I should live without thinking about it, I cannot do this because I have done it for too long already. Now I cannot help seeing the days and nights rushing toward me and leading me to death. I see only this, and this alone is truth. Everything else is a lie.

The two drops of honey which more than anything else had diverted my eyes from the cruel truth were my love for my family and my writing, which I referred to as art; yet this honey had lost its sweetness for me.

"My family . . . ," I said to myself. But my family, my wife and children, are people too. They are subject to the same conditions as I: they must either live in the lie or face the terrible truth. Why should they live? Why should I love them? Why care for them, bring them up, and watch over them? So that they can sink into the despair that eats away at me, or to turn them over to stupidity? If I love them, then I cannot hide the truth from them.

Every step they take in knowledge leads them to this truth. And the truth is death.

"Art, literature . . . ?" Under the influence of success and praise from others I had persuaded myself for a long time that this was something that may be done in spite of the approaching death that will annihilate everything—myself, my works, and the memory of them. But I soon saw that this, too, was a delusion. It became clear to me that art is an ornamentation of life, something that lures us into life. But life had lost its charm for me, so how was I to charm others? As long as I was not living my own life but the life of another that was carrying me along on its crest, as long as I believed that life had a meaning, even though I could not express it, the reflection of every kind of life through literature and the arts gave me pleasure; I enjoyed looking at life in the mirror of art. But when I began to search for the meaning of life, when I began to feel the need to live, this mirror became either tormenting or unnecessary, superfluous and ludicrous. It was no longer possible for me to be consoled by what I saw in the mirror, for I could see that my situation was stupid and despairing. It was good for me to rejoice when in the depths of my soul I believed that my life had meaning. Then this play of lights and shades, the play of the comical, the tragic, the moving, the beautiful, and the terrible elements in life had comforted me. But when I saw that life was meaningless and terrible the play in the mirror could no longer amuse me. No matter how sweet the honey, it could not be sweet to me, for I saw the dragon and the mice gnawing away at my support.

But it did not stop here. Had I simply understood that life has no meaning, I might have been able to calmly accept it; I might have recognized that such was my lot. But I could not rest content at this. Had I been like a man who lives in a forest from which he knows there is no way out, I might have been able to go on living; but I was like a man lost in the forest who was terrified by the fact that he was lost, like a man who was rushing about, longing to find his way and knowing that every step was leading him into deeper confusion, and yet who could not help rushing about.

This was the horror. And in order to be delivered from this horror, I wanted to kill myself. I felt a horror of what awaited me; I knew that this horror was more terrible than my present situation, but I could not keep it away and I did not have the patience to wait for the end. No matter how convincing the argument was that a blood vessel in the heart would burst anyway or that something else would rupture and it would be all over, I could not patiently await the end. The horror of the darkness was too great, and I wanted to be free of it as quickly as possible by means of a rope or a bullet. It was this feeling, more powerful than any other, that was leading me toward suicide.

V

Several times I asked myself, "Can it be that I have overlooked something, that there is something which I have failed to understand? Is it not possible that this state of despair is common to everyone?" And I searched for an answer to my questions in every area of knowledge acquired by man. For a long time I carried on my painstaking search; I did not search casually, out of mere curiosity, but painfully, persistently, day and night, like a dying man seeking salvation. I found nothing.

I searched all areas of knowledge, and not only did I fail to find anything, but I was convinced that all those who had explored knowledge as I did had also come up with nothing. Not only had they found nothing, but they had clearly acknowledged the same thing that had brought me to despair: the only absolute knowledge attainable by man is that life is meaningless.

I searched everywhere. And thanks to a life spent in study and to my connections with the learned world, I had access to the most learned from all the various fields of knowledge. These scholars did not refuse to reveal to me the sum of their knowledge, not only through their books but in conversations with them; I knew everything that knowledge had to answer to the question of life.

For a long time I could not bring myself to believe that knowledge had no reply to the question of life other than the one it had come up with. For a long time I thought I might have misunderstood something, as I closely observed the gravity and seriousness in the tone of science, convinced in its position, while having nothing to do with the question of human life. For a long time I was timid around knowledge, and I thought that the absurdity of the answers given to my questions was not the fault of knowledge but was due to my own ignorance; but the thing was that this to me was no joke, no game, but a matter of life and death; and I finally came to the conclusion that my questions were the only legitimate questions serving as a basis for all knowledge and that it was not I but science that was guilty before my questions if it should pretend to answer these questions.

My question, the question that had brought me to the edge of suicide when I was fifty years old, was the simplest question lying in the soul of every human being, from a silly child to the wisest of the elders, the question without which life is impossible; such was the way I felt about the matter. The question is this: What will come of what I do today and tomorrow? What will come of my entire life?

Expressed differently, the question may be: Why should I live? Why should I wish for anything or do anything? Or to put it still differently: Is there any meaning in my life that will not be destroyed by my inevitably approaching death?

Throughout human knowledge I sought an answer to this question, which is one and the same question in the various expressions of it. And I found that in regard to this question the sum of human knowledge is divided as if into two hemispheres lying opposite each other, into two opposite extremes occupying two poles, one positive and one negative. But there were no answers to the question of life at either pole.

One field of knowledge does not even acknowledge the question, even though it clearly and precisely answers the questions that it has posed independently. This is the field of experimental science, and at its extreme end is mathematics. The other field of knowledge acknowledges the questions but does not answer it. This is the field of speculative philosophy, and at its extreme end is metaphysics.

From my early youth I had studied speculative philosophy, but later both mathematics and the natural sciences attracted me. And until I had clearly put my question to myself, until the question itself grew within me and urgently demanded a resolution, I was satisfied with the counterfeit answers that knowledge had to offer.

In regard to the realm of experience, I said to myself, "Everything is developing and being differentiated, becoming more complex and moving toward perfection, and there are laws governing this process. You are part of the whole. If you learn as much as possible about the whole and if you learn the law of its development, you will come to know your place in the whole and to know yourself." As much as I am ashamed to admit it, there was a time when I seemed to be satisfied with this. It was at this time that I myself was developing and becoming more complex. My muscles were growing and getting stronger, my memory was being enriched, my ability to think and to comprehend was becoming greater; I was growing and developing. Feeling growth within me, it was natural for me to believe that perfectibility was indeed the law of the entire universe and that in this idea I would find the answers to the questions of my life. But the time came when I stopped growing; I felt that I was not growing but drying up. My muscles were growing weaker, my teeth were falling out, and I saw not only that this law explained nothing to me but that there never had been and never could be any law of this kind; I had merely mistaken something for a law which I happened to have found in myself at a particular time in my life. As I examined the nature of this law more closely, it became clear to me that there could be no such law of eternal development. It became clear to me that to say everything is developing, becoming more perfect, growing more complex and being differentiated in endless space and time amounted to saying nothing at all. None of these words has any meaning, for in the infinite there is nothing either simple or complex, nothing before or after, nothing better or worse.

The main thing was that my personal question, the question of what I am with all my desires, remained totally unanswered. I realized that these areas of knowledge may be very interesting and quite attractive, but their clarity and precision are inversely proportionate to their applicability to the questions of life. The less they have to do with the questions of life, the clearer and more precise they are; the more they attempt to provide answers to the questions of life, the more vague and unattractive they become. If we turn to those fields of knowledge that try to provide answers to the questions, to physiology, psychology, biology, sociology, then we encounter a striking poverty of thought and the greatest obscurity; we find in them a completely unjustified pretension to decide questions lying outside their scope, as well as incessant contradiction between one thinker and another and even thinkers contradicting themselves. If we turn to those fields of knowledge that are not concerned with answering the questions of life but only with answering their own special, scientific questions, then we may be carried away by the power of the human intellect, but we know beforehand that we shall find no answers to the question of life. These areas of knowledge completely ignore the question of life. They say, "We cannot tell you what you are and why you live; we do not have the answers to these questions, and we are not concerned with them. If you need to know about the laws of light, however, or about chemical compounds or the laws governing the development of organisms; if you need to know about the laws governing physical bodies, their forms and the relation between their size and number; if you need to know about the laws of your own mind, then for all this we have clear, precise, indubitable answers."

Generally the relation between the experimental sciences and the question of life may be expressed in this way: Question—Why do I live? Answer—In infinite space, in infinite time, infinitely small particles undergo modifications of infinite complexity, and when you understand the laws that govern these modifications, then you will understand why you live.

Then along more speculative lines I would say to myself, "All of mankind lives and develops according to the spiritual principles, according to the *ideals* that guide it. These ideals find expression in the religions, the sciences, the arts, and the forms of government. As these ideals rises higher and higher mankind proceeds on to its greater happiness. I am a part of mankind, and my

37

mission, therefore, lies in helping mankind through the consciousness and realization of these ideals." During my feeble-mindedness I was satisfied with this. But as soon as the question of life began to clearly emerge within me, this entire theory immediately collapsed. In addition to the careless inaccuracy with which this type of knowledge draws its conclusions and makes general claims about humanity after having studied only a small portion of it; in addition to the mutual contradiction among the various advocates of this view with respect to what the ideals of mankind are, the strangeness, if not the stupidity, of this view is that in order to answer the question that occurs to every man—"What am I?" or "Why do I live?" or "What am I to do?"—another question must first be settled: "What is the life of the humanity that is unknown to us, the life of which we can know only a small portion over a short period of time?" In order to know what he is, a man must first know what the sum of this mysterious humanity is, a humanity made up of people who, like himself, do not understand what they are.

I must confess that there was a time when I believed this. It was during the time when I had my own pet ideals to justify my whims, when I tried to devise one theory or another so that I could look upon my whims as laws that govern mankind. But as soon as the question of life began to emerge in my soul in all its clarity, this reply immediately crumbled into dust. And I realized that within the experimental sciences there are those that are genuinely scientific and those that are only half scientific, trying to give answers to questions that lie completely out of their realm; thus I realized that there is a whole series of the most widely diversified fields of knowledge that try to answer questions beyond their scope. Those that are only half scientific include the judicial, social, and historical sciences; in its own way each of these sciences attempts to decide the questions concerning the individual by seemingly deciding the question of life that concerns all of mankind.

But, as in the domain of the experimental sciences, a person who sincerely asks how he is to live cannot be satisfied with an answer that tells him to study the infinite complexities and changes that an infinite number of particles may go through in infinite space and time; in the same way, a sincere person cannot be satisfied with an answer that tells him to study the whole of humanity, whose beginning and end we cannot know and whose parts lie beyond our reach. It is the same with the semi-sciences as it is with the semi-experimental sciences: the more imbedded they are in obscurity, inaccuracy, stupidity, and contradiction, the further they deviate from their proper task. The task of experimental science is to determine the causal sequence of material phenomena. If experimental science should run into a question concerning an ultimate cause, it stumbles over nonsense. The task of speculative science is to discover the essence of life that lies beyond cause and effect. If its investigations should run into causal phenomena, such as social and historical phenomena, speculative science also stumbles over nonsense.

Experimental science, then, is concerned only with positive knowledge and reveals the greatness of the human intellect whenever its investigations do not enter into ultimate causes. And, on the other hand, speculative science reveals the greatness of the human intellect only when it completely removes all questions concerning the sequence of causal phenomena and examines man only in relation to an ultimate cause. Metaphysics or speculative philosophy occupies the extreme end of the spectrum of speculative sciences. This science clearly raises the question of what I am and what the universe is, the question of why I live and why the universe exists. And since its very beginning it has always answered in the same way. Whether the philosopher calls the essence of life that is within me and all living creatures an idea, a substance, a spirit, or a will, he is still saying that this essence exists and that *I* am this essence; but why it is there he does not know, and if he is a precise thinker, he does not answer. I ask, "Why does this essence exist, and what comes of the fact that it is and will be?" And not only does philosophy fail to answer, but all it can do itself is ask the same question. And if it is a true philosophy, then the sum of its labor lies in putting this question clearly. And if it holds firmly to its task, then it can have only one answer to the question of what I am and what the universe is: all and nothing. And to the question of why the universe exists and why I exist it can only reply: I do not know.

Thus no matter how I twist and turn the speculative answers of philosophy, I can obtain nothing resembling an answer; not because, as in the case of the clear, experimental sciences, the answer does not relate to my question, but because even though the sum of the intellectual labor is here directed toward my question, there is no answer. And instead of an answer, all one can obtain is the very same question put in a complicated form.

VI

In my search for answers to the question of life I felt exactly as a man who is lost in a forest.

I came to a clearing, climbed a tree, and had a clear view of the endless space around me. But I could see that there was no house and that there could be no house; I went into the thick of the forest, into the darkness, but again I could see no house—only darkness.

Thus I wandered about in the forest of human knowledge. On one side of me were the clearings of mathematical and experimental sciences, revealing to me sharp horizons; but in no direction could I see a house. On the other side of me was the darkness of the speculative sciences, where every step I took plunged me deeper into darkness, and I was finally convinced that there could be no way out.

When I gave myself over to the bright light of knowledge, I was only diverting my eyes from the question. However clear and tempting the horizons that opened up to me might have been, however tempting it was to sink into the infinity of this knowledge, I soon realized that the clearer this knowledge was, the less I needed it, the less it answered my question.

"Well," I said to myself, "I know everything that science wants so much to know, but this path will not lead me to an answer to the question of the meaning of my life." In the realm of speculative science I saw that in spite of—or rather precisely because of—the fact that this knowledge was designed to answer my question, there could be no answer other than the one I had given myself: What is the meaning of my life? It has none. Or: What will come of my life? Nothing. Or: Why does everything that is exist, and why do I exist? Because it exists.

From one branch of human knowledge I received an endless number of precise answers to questions I had not asked, answers concerning the chemical composition of the stars, the movement of the sun toward the constellation Hercules, the origin of the species and of man, the forms of infinitely small atoms, and the vibration of infinitely small and imponderable particles of ether. But the answer given by this branch of knowledge to my question about the meaning of my life was only this: you are what you call your life; you are a temporary, random conglomeration of particles. The thing that you have been led to refer to as your life is simply the mutual interaction and alteration of these particles. This conglomeration will continue for a certain period of time; then the interaction of these particles will come to a halt, and the thing you call your life will come to an end and with it all your questions. You are a little lump of something randomly stuck together. The lump decomposes. The decomposition of this lump is known as your life. The lump falls apart, and thus the decomposition ends, as do all your questions. Thus the clear side of knowledge replies, and if it strictly follows its own principles, there is no more to be said.

It turns out, however, that such an answer does not constitute a reply to the question. I must know the meaning of my life, but to say that it is a particle of infinity not only fails to give it any meaning but destroys all possible meaning.

The experimental, exact side of knowledge may strike some vague agreement with the speculative side, saying that the meaning of life lies in development and in the contributions made to this development. But given the innaccuracy and obscurity of such a remark, it cannot be regarded as an answer.

Whenever it holds strictly to its own principles in answering the question, the speculative side of knowledge has always come up with the same reply down through the centuries: the universe is something that is infinite and incomprehensible. Human life is an inscrutable part of this inscrutable "whole." Again I put aside all the agreements made between speculative and experimental knowledge that constitute the whole ballast of the semi-sciences, the so-called judicial, political, and historical sciences. In these sciences we are once again led to a false concept of development and perfection, with the only difference being that in one area we have the development of everything and in the other the development of people. The falsehood is the same in both cases: development and perfection can have no purpose in infinity, no direction, and therefore can give no answer to my question.

Wherever speculative knowledge is exact and may be called true philosophy, and not what Schopenhauer refers to as professorial philosophy, which serves only to divide all existing phenomena into new philosophical columns with new names; wherever philosophy does not turn away from the essential question, the answer is always the same as the one given by Socrates, Schopenhauer, Solomon, and the Buddha.

"We move closer to the truth only to the extent that we move further from life," says Socrates, as he prepares for death. What do we who love truth strive for in life? To be free of the body and of all the evils that result from the life of the body. If this is so, then how can we fail to rejoice when death approaches?

"The wise man seeks death all his life, and for this reason death is not terrifying to him."*

"If we accept the inner essence of the universe as will," says Schopenhauer, "and if we accept the objectivity of this will in all phenomena, from the unconscious surges of the dark forces of nature to the fully conscious activity of man, we cannot avoid the conclusion that all these phenomena disappear in the free denial and self-annihilation of will; the constant striving, the aimless and restless inclination toward all the levels of objectivity that make up the universe will disappear, and the variety of successive forms will come to an end; and when form disappears, so do all the phenomena of form, including space and time, until the ultimate foundation of form finally disappears, that of subject and object. Where there is no will, no appearance of phenomena, there is no universe. The only thing that remains before us is, of course,

*Socrates (470–399 B.C.) discusses this in Sections 62–69 of Plato's *Phaedo*, when his friends have come to see him one last time before his appointed execution.

nothingness. But the thing that opposes this passage into nothingness is our nature, our own will to live *(Wille zum Leben)*, by which we are constituted, as is our universe. The fact that we are so frightened of nothingness, or that we long so to live only signifies that we ourselves are merely this desire to live, and that we know nothing except this desire. Therefore, upon the complete annihilation of the will, all that remains for us, we who are fulfilled by that will, is, of course, nothingness; but on the other hand, for those in whom the will has been transformed and renounced, this universe of ours which is so real, with all its suns and galaxies, *is itself nothingness.*"*

"Vanity of vanities," says Solomon, "vanity of vanities, all is vanity! What profit does a man derive from all the labors by which he toils under the sun? One generation comes, while another generation passes away; but the earth abides forever. What has been will be; what has been done will be done; and there is nothing new under the sun. Is there anything of which it may be said, behold, this is new? No, it has been already in the centuries that have come before us. There is no remembrance of former things; and there will be no remembrance of the things to come on the part of those who come afterward. I, the Preacher, was King over Israel in Jerusalem. And I gave up my heart to search and seek out through wisdom all the things that are under the sun; this hard pursuit God has given to the sons of men, so that they may be exercised in it. I have seen all things that are done under the sun, and behold, all is vanity and a languishing of the spirit. . . . I spoke in my heart, saying, see how I have been exalted and have attained more wisdom than all who have ruled over Jerusalem before me.

*Arthur Schopenhauer (1788–1860) had a profound influence on Tolstoy's thinking, especially during the time when he was writing *War and Peace*. The concepts presented here are found in Schopenhauer's *Parerga and Paralipomena*.

And my heart held much wisdom and knowledge. And I gave my heart over to knowing wisdom and to knowing madness and folly; I discovered that this too is a languishing of the spirit. For in much wisdom is much grief, and he who increases wisdom increases sorrow.

"I spoke in my heart, saying, I will try you with mirth, and you will enjoy the pleasures of good things; but this too is vanity. Of laughter I said: it is foolishness; and of mirth: what does it do? I thought in my heart to delight my body with wine, and though my heart was guided by wisdom, I thought to adhere to foolishness until I could see what was good for the sons of men and discover what they should do under heaven during the few days of their lives. I undertook great deeds: I erected buildings and planted vineyards for myself. I set up gardens and orchards and planted every kind of fruit-bearing tree; I made reservoirs to water the orchards, so that the trees might spring up. I acquired servants and maidservants, and there were servants born in my house; I also had cattle, great and small, more than any who had been in Jerusalem before me; I obtained silver and gold and treasures from kings and from other regions; I gathered unto myself singers and women who sing and the delights of the sons of men and various musical instruments. And I became greater and wealthier than all who had ruled Jerusalem before me; and my wisdom abided with me. Whatever my eyes desired I kept not from them, nor did I forbid my heart any delight. And I looked around at all the deeds my hands had performed and at the labors by which I had toiled; and behold, all was vanity and a languishing of the spirit, and there was no profit from them under the sun. And I turned about to look upon wisdom and madness and foolishness. But I found that one lot fell to them all. And in my heart I said: the same lot will fall to me as to the fool—why, then, had I become so wise? And I said to my heart: this too is vanity. For there will be no eternal memory of the wise man or of the fool; in the days to come all will be forgotten, and alas, the wise man dies the same death as the fool! And I came to hate life, because all the works that are done under the sun had become repulsive to me; for all is vanity and a languishing of the spirit. And I came to hate the labor by which I had toiled under the sun, because it must be left to the man who will come after me. For what will a man have from all his labor and the anxieties of his heart by which he toils under the sun? For all his days are sorrow and his labors grief; even at night his heart does not know peace. And this too is vanity. There is nothing better for a man than to eat and drink and let his soul find delight in his labor. . . .

"All things come alike to all; one lot falls to the righteous and to the wicked, to the good and to the evil, to the clean and to the unclean, to the one who sacrifices and to the one who does not sacrifice; as to the virtuous, so to the sinner; as to the one who swears, so to the one who fears an oath. This is an evil among all things that are done under the sun, that one lot falls to all, and that the heart of the sons of men is full of evil, that there is madness in their heart and in their life; and after this they go to join the dead. Whoever is among the living still has hope, since it is better to be a living dog than a dead lion. The living know that they will die, but the dead know nothing, neither have they any reward, for even the memory of them has been lost to forgetfulness; their love, their hate, and their jealousy have already vanished, and there will be no more honor done to them in all the things that are done under the sun."*

Thus speaks Solomon, or the one who has written these words.

*The passages here cited by Tolstoy are from the Book of Ecclesiastes, which was not actually written by Solomon, who died around 930 B.C., but rather dates from the third century B.C.

And this is what an Indian sage has to say:

Sakia-Muni, a young and happy prince from whom sickness, old age, and death had been hidden, went out for a ride one day and saw a dreadful, toothless, driveling old man. The prince, from whom until now old age had been hidden, was taken aback and asked the driver what this meant and why this man had come to such a pitiful, disgusting, hideous state. And when he found out that this is the common lot of all people, that he, the young prince, would also come to this, he could not go on with the drive and ordered the driver to return home so that he could reflect on this. And he shut himself up alone and pondered it. He probably thought of something or other to console him, for once again, happy and cheerful, he went out for a drive. But this time he met a sick man. He saw an emaciated, feeble, trembling man with dim eyes. The prince, from whom sickness had been hidden, stopped and asked what this could mean. And when he found out that this was sickness, which befalls all people, and that even he, the healthy and happy prince, may get sick tomorrow, once again the spirit of merriment left him; he ordered the driver to return home, where he again sought peace of mind. And he probably found it, for a third time he went out for a drive. But the third time he saw yet another new sight; he saw some people carrying something. "What is it?" A dead man. "What does dead mean?" asked the prince. And he was told that to become a dead man means to become what this man had become. The prince went down to the dead man, uncovered him and looked at him. "And what now will become of him?" asked the prince. And he was told that the man would be buried in the earth. "Why?" Because he will never again be alive, and only stench and worms will come of him. "And this is the fate of all people? And it will happen to me as well? They will bury me, and a stench will rise from me, and worms will consume me?" Yes. "Go back! I don't want to go for a drive, I shall never go for a drive again."

Sakia-Muni could find no comfort in life. He decided that life is a great evil, and he drew on all the strength of his soul to free himself and others from life, to free them in such a way that after death life would never be renewed and the root of life would be completely destroyed. Thus speak all the Indian sages.

Thus we have the direct answers that human wisdom has to give when it answers the question of life.

"The life of the body is an evil and a lie. And so the destruction of the life of the body is a blessing, and we should long for it," says Socrates.

"Life is what it should not be, an evil; and a passage into nothingness is the only blessing that life has to offer," says Schopenhauer.

"Everything in the world—both folly and wisdom, wealth and poverty, joy and sorrow—all is vanity and emptiness. A man dies and nothing remains. And this is absurd," says Solomon.

"It is not possible to live, knowing that suffering, decrepitness, old age, and death are inevitable; we must free ourselves from life and from all possibility of life," says the Buddha.

And the very thing that has been uttered by these powerful minds has been said, thought, and felt by millions of people like them. I too have thought and felt the same way.

Thus my wanderings among the fields of knowledge not only failed to lead me out of my despair but rather increased it. One area of knowledge did not answer the question of life; the other branch of knowledge did indeed answer, all the more confirming my despair and showing me that the thing that had befallen me was not due to an error on my part or to a sick state of mind. On the contrary, this area of knowledge confirmed for me the fact that I had been thinking correctly and had been in agreement with the most powerful minds known to humanity.

I could not be deceived. All is vanity. Happy is he who has never been born; death is better than life; we must rid ourselves of life.

VII

Having failed to find an explanation in knowledge, I began to look for it in life, hoping to find it in the people around me. And so I began to observe people like myself to see how they lived and to determine what sort of relation they had with the question that had led me to despair.

And this is what I found among people whose circumstances were precisely the same as mine with respect to education and way of life.

I found that for the people of my class there were four means of escaping the terrible situation in which we all find ourselves.

The first means of escape is that of ignorance. It consists of failing to realize and to understand that life is evil and meaningless. For the most part, people in this category are women, or they are very young or very stupid men; they still have not understood the problem of life that presented itself to Schopenhauer, Solomon, and the Buddha. They see neither the dragon that awaits them nor the mice gnawing away at the branch they cling to; they simply lick the drops of honey. But they lick these drops of honey only for the time being; something will turn their attention toward the dragon and the mice, and there will be an end to their licking. There was nothing for me to learn from them, since we cannot cease to know what we know.

The second escape is that of epicureanism. Fully aware of the hopelessness of life, it consists of enjoying for the present the blessings that we do have without looking at the dragon or the mice; it lies in licking the honey as best we can, especially in those places where there is the most honey on the bush. Solomon describes this escape in the following manner:

"And I commended mirth, for there is nothing better for man under the sun than to eat, drink, and be merry; this will be his mainstay in his toil through the days of his life that God has given him under the sun.

"So go and eat your bread with joy and drink your wine in the gladness of your heart. . . . Enjoy life with a *woman* you love through all the days of your life of vanity, through all your vain days; for this is your fate in life and in the labors by which you toil under the sun. . . . Do whatever you can do by the strength of your hand, for there is no work in the grave where you are going, no reflection, no knowledge, no wisdom."

Most people of our class pursue this second means of escape. The situation in which they find themselves is such that it affords them more of the good things in life than the bad; their moral stupidity enables them to forget that all the advantages of their position are accidental, that not everyone can have a thousand women and palaces, as Solomon did; they forget that for every man with a thousand wives there are a thousand men without wives, that for every palace there are a thousand men who built it by the sweat of their brows, and that the same chance that has made them a Solomon today might well make them Solomon's slave tomorrow. The dullness of the imagination of these people enables them to forget what left the Buddha with no peace: the inevitability of sickness, old age, and death, which if not today then tomorrow will destroy all these pleasures. The fact that some of these people maintain that their dullness of thought and imagination is positive philosophy does not, in my opinion, distinguish them from those who lick the honey without seeing the problem. I could not imitate these people, since I did not lack imagination and could not pretend that I did. Like every man who truly lives, I could not turn my eyes away from the mice and the dragon once I had seen them.

The third means of escape is through strength and energy. It consists of destroying life once one has realized that life is evil and meaningless. Only unusually strong and logically consistent people act in this manner. Having realized all the stupidity of the joke that is being played on us and seeing that the blessings of the dead are greater than those of the living and that it is better not to exist, they act and put an end to this stupid joke; and they use any means of doing it: a rope around the neck, water, a knife in the heart, a train. There are more and more people of our class who are acting in this way. For the most part, the people who perform these acts are in the very prime of life, when the strength of the soul is at its peak and when the habits that undermine human reason have not yet taken over. I saw that this was the most worthy means of escape, and I wanted to take it.

The fourth means of escape is that of weakness. It consists of continuing to drag out a life that is evil and meaningless, knowing beforehand that nothing can come of it. The people in this category know that death is better than life, but they do not have the strength to act rationally and quickly put an end to the delusion by killing themselves; instead they seem to be waiting for something to happen. This is the escape of weakness, for if I know what is better and have it within my reach, then why not surrender myself to it? I myself belonged in this category.

Thus the people of my class save themselves from a terrible contradiction in these four ways. No matter how much I strained my intellectual faculties, I could see no escape other than these four. One escape lies in failing to realize that life is meaningless, vain, and evil, and that it is better not to live. It was impossible for me not to know this, and once I had discovered the truth I could not close my eyes to it. Another escape lies in making use of whatever life has to offer without thinking about the future. And this I could not do. Like Sakia-Muni, I could find no pleasure in life once I had come to know what old age, suffering, and death are. My imagination was too active. Moreover, I could not enjoy the transient pleasures that just happened to come my way for a moment. The third escape lies in knowing that life is evil and absurd and putting an end to it by killing yourself. I understood this, but for some reason I did not kill myself. The fourth means of escape lies in knowing that life is as Solomon and Schopenhauer have described it, knowing that it is a stupid joke being played on us, and yet continuing to live, to wash, dress, dine, talk, and even write books. Such a position was disgusting and painful to me, but I remained in it all the same.

Now I see that if I did not kill myself, it was because I had some vague notion that my ideas were all wrong. However convincing and unquestionable the train of my thoughts and of the thoughts of the wise seemed to me, the ideas that had led us to affirm the meaninglessness of life, I still had some obscure doubt about the point of departure of my reflections.

My doubt was expressed in this way: I, that is, my reason declared that life is irrational. If there is nothing higher than reason (and there is no way to prove that there is anything higher than it), then reason is the creator of life for me. If there were no reason, then for me there would be no life. So how can this reason deny life when it is itself the creator of life? Or to put it differently: if there were no life, my reason would not exist either. Therefore, reason is the offspring of life. Life is all. Reason is the fruit of life, and yet this reason denies that very life. I felt that something was wrong here.

"Life is an absurd evil; there is no doubting this," I said to myself. "But I have lived, and I am still living; and all of humanity has lived and continues to live. How can this be? Why do men live when they are able to die? Can it be that Schopenhauer and I are the only ones brilliant enough to have realized that life is meaningless and evil?"

Understanding the vanity of life is not so difficult, and even the simplest of people have understood it for a long time; yet they have lived and continue to live. How is it that they all go on living and never think to doubt the rationality of life?

My acquired knowledge, confirmed by the wisdom of the wisest of men, revealed to me that everything in the world, both organic and inorganic, was arranged with extraordinary intelligence; my position alone was absurd. But these fools, the huge masses of simple people, know nothing about the organic and inorganic arrangement of the world, and yet they live, all the while believing that life is arranged in a very rational manner!

It occurred to me that there still might be something that I did not know. After all, ignorance acts precisely in this manner. Ignorance always says exactly what I was saying. Whenever it does not know something, it says that whatever it does not know is stupid. It really comes down to this: all of mankind has lived and continues to live as if it knew the meaning of life, for without knowing the meaning of life it could not live; but I am saying that all this life is meaningless and that I cannot live.

No one prevents us from denying life, as Schopenhauer has done. So kill yourself, and you won't have to worry about it. If you don't like life, kill yourself. If you live and cannot understand the meaning of life, put an end to it; but don't turn around and start talking and writing about how you don't understand life. You are in cheerful company, for whom everything is going well, and they all know what they are doing; if you are bored and find it offensive, leave.

After all, if we are convinced of the necessity of suicide and do not go through with it, then what are we, if not the weakest, most inconsistent, and, to speak quite frankly, the most stupid of all people, fussing like foolish children over a new toy?

After all, our wisdom, however accurate it may be, has not provided us with an understanding of the meaning of life. Yet the millions who make up the sum of humanity take part in life without ever doubting the meaning of life.

Indeed, since ancient times, when the life of which I do know something began, people who knew the arguments concerning the vanity of life, the arguments that revealed to me its meaninglessness, lived nonetheless, bringing to life a meaning of their own. Since the time when people somehow began to live, this meaning of life has been with them, and they have led this life up to my own time. Everything that is in me and around me is the fruit of their knowledge of life. The very tools of thought by which I judge life and condemn it were created not by me but by them. I myself was born, educated and have grown up thanks to them. They dug out the iron, taught us how to cut the timber, tamed the cattle and the horses, showed us how to sow crops and live together; they brought order to our lives. They taught me how to think and to speak. I am their offspring, nursed by them, reared by them, taught by them; I think according to their thoughts, their words, and now I have proved to them that it is all meaningless! "Something is wrong here," I said to myself. "I must have made a mistake somewhere." But I looked and looked and could not find where the mistake could be.

VIII

All these doubts, which I am now in a position to express more or less clearly, I was then unable to express. I simply felt that no matter how logically inescapable my conclusions about the vanity of life might have been, there was something wrong with them, even though they had been confirmed by the greatest of thinkers. Whether it was my thinking or my formulation of the question, I did not know. I only felt that as convinced as my reason might have been, this was not enough. All of these arguments could not persuade me to follow my thinking to its logical end, that is, to kill myself. I would not be speaking the truth if I were to say that it was through reason that I had arrived at this point without killing myself. Reason was at work, but there was something else at work too, something I can only call a consciousness of life. There was also a force at work that had led me to focus my attention on one thing instead of another; it was this force that brought me out of my despairing situation, and it took a direction that is completely foreign to reason. This force led me to focus my attention on the fact that like hundreds of other people of my class I was not the whole of humanity, and that I still did not know what the life of humanity was.

As I looked about the narrow circle of my peers I saw only people who did not understand the problem, people who understood it but drowned it their intoxication with life, people who understood it and put an end to life, and people who understood it but out of weakness continued to live a life of despair. That was all I could see. I thought that this narrow circle of learned, wealthy, and idle people to which I belonged comprised the sum of mankind and that the millions who had lived and continued to live outside of this circle were *animals,* not people.

How strange and utterly incredible it seems to me now that in my reasoning I could have overlooked the life of humanity all around me, that I could have fallen into such a ridiculous state of error as to think that my life and the life of a Solomon or a Schopenhauer was the true, normal life, while the lives of millions of others were not worthy of consideration; but however strange it may seem to me now, such was the case at that time. Led astray by intellectual pride, I thought there could be no doubt that along with Solomon and Schopenhauer, I had posed the question so precisely, so truthfully, that there were no two ways about it; I thought there could be no doubt that all these millions were among those who had never penetrated the depths of the question. As I searched for the meaning of my life it never once occurred to me to ask, "What sort of meaning do the millions in the world who have lived and who now live ascribe to their lives?"

For a long time I lived in this state of madness which, if not in word then in deed, is especially pronounced among the most liberal and most learned of men. I do not know whether it was due to the strange sort of instinctive love I had for the working people that I was compelled to understand them and to see that they are not as stupid as we think; or whether it was my sincere conviction that I knew nothing better to do than to hang myself that led me to realize this: if I wanted to live and to understand the meaning of life, I had to seek this meaning not among those who have lost it and want to destroy themselves but among the millions of people, living and dead, who created life and took upon themselves the burden of their lives as well as our own. So I looked around at the huge masses of simple people, living and dead, who were neither learned nor wealthy, and I saw something quite different. I saw that all of these millions of people who have lived and still live did not fall into my category, with only a few rare exceptions. I could not regard them as people who did not understand the question because they themselves put the question with unusual clarity and answered it. Nor could I regard them as Epicureans, since their lives are marked more by deprivation and suffering than by pleasure. And even less could I regard them as people who carried on a meaningless life in an irrational manner, since they could explain every act of their lives, even death itself. And they looked upon killing oneself as the greatest of evils. It turned out that all of humanity had some kind of knowledge of the meaning of life which I had overlooked and held in contempt. It followed that rational knowledge does not give meaning to life, that it excludes life; the meaning that millions of people give to life is based on some kind of knowledge that is despised and considered false.

As presented by the learned and the wise, rational knowledge denies the meaning of life, but the huge masses of people acknowledge meaning through an irrational knowledge. And this irrational knowledge is faith, the one thing that I could not accept. This involves the God who is both one and three, the creation in six days, devils, angels and everything else that I could not accept without taking leave of my senses.

My position was terrible. I knew that I could find nothing in the way of rational knowledge except a denial of life; and in faith I could find nothing except a denial of reason, and this was even more impossible than a denial of life. According to rational knowledge, it followed that life is evil, and people know it. They do not have to live, yet they have lived and they do live, just as I myself had lived, even though I had known for a long time that life is meaningless and evil. According to faith, it followed that in order to understand the meaning of life I would have to turn away from reason, the very thing for which meaning was necessary.

IX

I ran into a contradiction from which there were only two ways out: either the thing that I had referred to as reason was not as rational as I had thought, or the thing that I took to be irrational was not as irrational as I had thought. And I began to examine the course of the arguments that had come of my rational knowledge.

As I looked more closely at this course, I found it to be entirely correct. The conclusion that life is nothing was unavoidable; but I detected a mistake. The mistake was that my thinking did not correspond to the question I had raised. The question was: Why should I live? Or: Is there anything real and imperishable that will come of my illusory and perishable life? Or: What kind of meaning can my finite existence have in this infinite universe? In order to answer this question, I studied life.

It was obvious that the resolution of all the possible questions of life could not satisfy me because my question, no matter how simple it may seem at first glance, entails a demand to explain the finite by means of the infinite and the infinite by means of the finite.

I asked, "What is the meaning of my life beyond space, time, and causation?" And I answered, "What is the meaning of my life within space, time, and causation?" After a long time spent in the labor of thought, it followed that I could reply only that my life had no meaning at all.

Throughout my reasoning I was constantly comparing the finite to the finite and the infinite to the infinite; indeed, I could not do otherwise. Thus I concluded and had to conclude that force is force, matter is matter, will is will, infinity is infinity, nothing is nothing; and I could not get beyond that.

It was something similar to what happens in mathematics when we are trying to figure out how to solve an equation and all we can get is an identity. The method for solving the equation is correct, but all we get for an answer is $a = a$, or $x = x$, or $0 = 0$. The same thing was happening with my reasoning in regard to the question concerning the significance of my life. The answers that all the sciences give to this question are only identities.

And in reality a strictly rational knowledge begins, in the manner of Descartes, with an absolute doubt of everything.* Strictly rational knowledge casts aside any knowledge based on faith and reconstructs everything anew according to the laws of reason and experiment; it can give no answer to the question of life other than the one I had received—an indefinite one. It seemed to me only at first that knowledge gave a positive answer, the answer of Schopenhauer: life has no meaning, it is an evil. But as I looked into the matter I realized that this is not a positive answer and that only my emotions had taken it to be so. Strictly expressed, as it is expressed by the Brahmins,† by Solomon, and by Schopenhauer, the answer is only a vague one or an identity; $0 = 0$, life that presents itself to me as nothing is nothing. Thus philosophical knowledge denies nothing but merely replies that it

*René Descartes (1596–1650) is often referred to as the father of modern philosophy. He begins one of his most famous works, the *Meditations on First Philosophy*, from a position of absolute doubt, a principle he also discusses in the *Discourse on Method*.
†Brahmins are Hindus of the highest caste, traditionally assigned to the priesthood.

cannot decide this question and that from its point of view any resolution remains indefinite.

Having understood this, I realized that I could not search for an answer to my question in rational knowledge. The answer given by rational knowledge is merely an indication that an answer can be obtained only by formulating the question differently, that is, only when the relationship between the finite and the infinite is introduced into the question. I also realized that no matter how irrational and unattractive the answers given by faith, they have the advantage of bringing to every reply a relationship between the finite and the infinite, without which there can be no reply. However I may put the question of how I am to live, the answer is: according to the law of God. Is there anything real that will come of my life? Eternal torment or eternal happiness. What meaning is there which is not destroyed by death? Union with the infinite God, paradise.

Thus in addition to rational knowledge, which before had seemed to be the only knowledge, I was inevitably led to recognize a different type of knowledge, an irrational type, which all of humanity had: faith, which provides us with the possibility of living. As far as I was concerned, faith was as irrational as ever, but I could not fail to recognize that it alone provides humanity with an answer to the question of life, thus making it possible to live.

Rational knowledge led me to the conclusion that life is meaningless; my life came to a halt, and I wanted to do away with myself. As I looked around at people, I saw that they were living, and I was convinced that they knew the meaning of life. Then I turned and looked at myself; as long as I knew the meaning of life, I lived. As it was with others, so it was with me: faith provided me with the meaning of life and the possibility of living.

Upon a further examination of the people in other countries, of my contemporaries, and of those who have passed away, I saw the same thing. Wherever there is life, there is faith; since the origin of mankind faith has made it possible for us to live, and the main characteristics of faith are everywhere and always the same.

No matter what answers a given faith might provide for us, every answer of faith gives infinite meaning to the finite existence of man, meaning that is not destroyed by suffering, deprivation, and death. Therefore, the meaning of life and the possibility of living may be found in faith alone. I realized that the essential significance of faith lies not only in the "manifestation of things unseen" and so on, or in revelation (this is simply a description of one of the signs of faith); nor is it simply the relation between man and God (faith must first be determined and then God, not the other way around), or agreeing with what one has been told, even though this is what it is most often understood to be. Faith is the knowledge of the meaning of human life, whereby the individual does not destroy himself but lives. Faith is the force of life. If a man lives, then he must have faith in something. If he did not believe that he had something he must live for, then he would not live. If he fails to see and understand the illusory nature of the finite, then he believes in the finite; if he understands the illusory nature of the finite, then he must believe in the infinite. Without faith it is impossible to live.

I looked back on the course of my internal life and I was horrified. It was now clear to me that in order for a man to live, he must either fail to see the infinite or he must have an explanation of the meaning of life by which the finite and the infinite would be equated. I had such an explanation, but I did not need it as long as I believed in the finite, and I began to use reason to test it out. And in the light of reason every bit of my former explanation crumbled into dust. But the time came when I no longer believed in the finite. And then, using the foundations of reason, I began to draw on what I knew to put together an explanation that would give life meaning; but nothing came of it. Along with the finest minds that mankind has produced, I came up with o = o, and I was utterly amazed at coming to such a resolution and at discovering that there could be no other.

And what did I do when I searched for an answer in the experimental sciences? I wanted to find out why I lived, and to do that I studied everything that was outside of myself. To be sure, I was able to learn a great deal, but nothing of what I needed.

And what did I do when I searched for an answer in the area of philosophy? I studied the thoughts of those who found themselves in the same situation as I, and they had no answer to the question of why I live. I was not able to learn anything here that I did not already know—namely, that it is impossible to know anything.

What am I? A part of the infinite. Indeed, in these words lies the whole problem. Is it possible that man has only now raised this question? And can it be that no one before me has put this question to himself, a question so simple that it rests on the tip of the tongue of every intelligent child?

No, this question has been asked ever since there have been people to ask it; since the beginning man has understood that to resolve the question by equating the finite with the finite is just as inadequate as equating the infinite with the infinite; since the beginning man has sought to articulate the relation between the finite and the infinite.

We subject to logical inquiry all the concepts that identify the finite with the infinite and through which we receive the meaning of life and the ideas of God, freedom, and good. And these concepts do not stand up to the critiques born of reason.

If it were not so terrible, it would be laughable to see the pride and complacency with which, like children, we take apart the watch, removing the spring and making a plaything of it, only to be surprised when the watch stops running.

A resolution of the contradiction between the finite and the infinite, an answer to the question of life that makes it possible to live, is necessary and dear to us. And the one resolution that we find everywhere, at all times and among all nations, is the resolution that has come down from a time in which all human life is lost to us. It is a resolution so difficult that we could come up with nothing like it, one that we thoughtlessly undo by again raising the question that occurs to everyone and for which we have no answer.

The concepts of an infinite God, moral good and evil, the immortality of the soul, and a relation between God and the affairs of man are ones that have been worked out historically through the life of a humanity that is hidden from our eyes. They are concepts without which there would be no life, without which I myself could not live, and yet, putting aside all the labor of humankind, I wanted to do it all over again by myself and in my own way.

I did not think so at the time, but even then the seeds of these thoughts had already been planted within me. I realized first of all that despite our wisdom, the position of Schopenhauer, Solomon, and myself was absurd: we considered life evil, and yet we lived. This is clearly absurd because if life is meaningless and if I love reason so much, then I must destroy life so there will be no one around to deny it. Secondly, I realized that all our arguments went round and round in a vicious circle, like a cog whose gears are out of sync. No matter how refined our reasoning, we could not come up with an answer; it would always turn out that $0 = 0$, and our method was therefore probably mistaken. Finally,

I began to realize that the most profound wisdom of man was rooted in the answers given by faith and that I did not have the right to deny them on the grounds of reason; above all, I realized that these answers alone can form a reply to the question of life.

X

I understood this, but it did not make things any easier for me. I was now prepared to accept any faith, as long as it did not demand of me a direct denial of reason, for such a denial would be a lie. So I studied the texts of Buddhism and Muhammadanism; and more than ever those of Christianity and the lives of Christians who lived around me.

Naturally, I turned first of all to believers from my own class —people of learning, Orthodox theologians, elder monks, progressive Orthodox theologians, and even the so-called New Christians, who professed salvation through faith in redemption. I seized upon these believers and questioned them about what they believed and how they viewed the meaning of life.

In spite of the fact that I made every possible concession and avoided all arguments, I could not accept the faith of these people. I saw that what they took to be faith did not explain the meaning of life but only obscured it, and that they themselves professed their faith not in response to the question of life that had drawn me to faith but for some purpose that was alien to me.

I remember the agonizing feeling of horror upon returning to my original despair, which followed the hope I had felt so many times in my relations with these people. The more they laid their teachings before me in ever-increasing detail, the more clearly I could see their error, until I lost all hope of discovering in their faith any explanation of the meaning of life.

I was not alienated so much by the fact that in presenting their beliefs they would mix the Christian truths that had always been so dear to me with much that was superfluous and irrational. Rather, it was that their lives were so much like my own, but with this one difference: they did not live according to the principles they professed. I felt very strongly that they were deceiving themselves and that, like myself, they had no sense of life's meaning other than to live while they lived and to lay their hands on everything they could. This was clear to me because if they harbored any meaning that might destroy all fear of privation, suffering, and death, they would not be frightened of these things. But these believers from our class lived a life of plenty, just as I did; they endeavored to increase and preserve their wealth and were afraid of privation, suffering, death. Like myself and all the rest of us unbelievers, they lived only to satisfy their lusts, lived just as badly as, if not worse than, those who did not believe.

No rationalization could convince me of the truth of their faith, though one thing might have: actions proving that these people held the key to a meaning of life that would eliminate in them the fear of poverty, sickness, and death that haunted me. But I saw no trace of such actions among the various believers in our class. On the contrary, I saw such actions among people in our class who were not believers but never among the so-called believers.

Thus I realized that the faith of these people was not the faith I sought, that their faith was not faith at all but only one of the epicurean gratifications in life. I realized that while this faith may not console, it might serve to dispel the remorse of a Solomon on his deathbed; but it is of no use to the overwhelming majority of humankind, those who are called not to amuse themselves at the expense of the labors of others but to create life. In order for all humankind to live, to sustain life and instill it with meaning, these millions must all have a different, more genuine concept of faith. Indeed, it was not that Solomon, Schopenhauer, and I did not kill ourselves that convinced me of the existence of faith but that these millions have lived and continue to live, carrying the Solomons and me on the waves of their lives.

And I began to grow closer to the believers from among the poor, the simple, the uneducated folk, from among the pilgrims, the monks, the Raskolniks,* the peasants. The beliefs of those from among the people, like those of the pretentious believers from our class, were Christian. Here too there was much superstition mixed in with the truths of Christianity, but with this difference: the superstitions of the believers from our class were utterly unnecessary to them, played no role in their lives, and were only a kind of epicurean diversion, while the superstitions of the believers from the laboring people were intertwined with their lives to such a degree that their lives could not be conceived without them: their superstitions were a necessary condition for their lives. The whole life of the believers from our class was in opposition to their faith, while the whole life of the believers from the working people was a confirmation of that meaning of life which was the substance of their faith. So I began to examine the life and the teachings of these people, and the closer I looked, the more I was convinced that theirs was the true faith, that their faith was indispensable to them and that this faith alone provided them with the meaning and possibility of life. Contrary to what I saw among the people of our class, where life was possible without

*Raskolniks were "dissenters" from the Russian Orthodox Church and members of any one of several groups, including the Doukhobors and the Khlysty, which arose as a result of the schism of the seventeenth century in protest against liturgical reforms; they are sometimes referred to as Old Believers.

faith and scarcely one in a thousand was a believer, among these people there was scarcely one in a thousand who was not a believer. Contrary to what I saw among the people of our class, where a lifetime is passed in idleness, amusement, and dissatisfaction with life, these people spent their lives at hard labor and were less dissatisfied with life than the wealthy. Contrary to the people of our class who resist and are unhappy with the hardship and suffering of their lot, these people endure sickness and tribulation without question or resistance—peacefully, and in the firm conviction that this is as it should be, cannot be otherwise, and is good. Contrary to the fact that the greater our intellect, the less we understand the meaning of life and the more we see some kind of evil joke in our suffering and death, these people live, suffer, and draw near to death peacefully and, more often than not, joyfully. Contrary to peaceful death—death without horror and despair, which is the rarest exception in our class—it is the tormenting, unyielding, and sorrowful death that is the rarest exception among the people. And these people, who are deprived of everything that for Solomon and me constituted the only good in life, yet who nonetheless enjoy the greatest happiness, form the overwhelming majority of mankind. I looked further still around myself. I examined the lives of the great masses of people who have lived in the past and live today. Among those who have understood the meaning of life, who know how to live and die, I saw not two or three or ten but hundreds, thousands, millions. And all of them, infinitely varied in their customs, intellects, educations, and positions and in complete contrast to my ignorance, knew the meaning of life and death, labored in peace, endured suffering and hardship, lived and died, and saw in this not vanity but good.

I grew to love these people. The more I learned about the lives of those living and dead about whom I had read and heard, the more I loved them and the easier it became for me to live. I lived this way for about two years, and a profound transformation came over me, one that had been brewing in me for a long time and whose elements had always been a part of me. The life of our class, of the wealthy and the learned, was not only repulsive to me but had lost all meaning. The sum of our action and thinking, of our science and art, all of it struck me as the overindulgences of a spoiled child. I realized that meaning was not to be sought here. The actions of the laboring people, of those who create life, began to appear to me as the one true way. I realized that the meaning provided by this life was truth, and I embraced it.

XI

When I remembered how these very beliefs had repelled me and seemed meaningless in the mouths of people who led lives in contradiction to them, and when I recalled how the same beliefs attracted me and seemed sensible as I saw people who lived by them, I realized why I had once turned away from them and had found them meaningless, while now I was drawn to them and found them full of meaning. I realized that I had lost my way and how I had lost my way. My straying had resulted not so much from wrong thinking as from bad living. I realized that the truth had been hidden from me not so much because my thoughts were in error as because my life itself had been squandered in the satisfaction of lusts, spent under the exceptional conditions of epicureanism. I realized that in asking, "What is my life?" and then answering, "An evil," I was entirely correct. The error lay in the fact that I had taken an answer that applied only to myself and applied it to life in general; I had asked myself what my life was and received the reply: evil and meaningless. And so it was: my life, wasted in the indulgence of lusts, was meaningless and evil, and the assertion that life is meaningless and evil thus applied only to my life and not to life in general. I understood the truth that I later found in the Gospel, the truth that people clung to darkness and shunned the light because their deeds were evil. For he who does evil hates the light and will not venture into the light, lest his deeds be revealed. I realized that in order to understand the meaning of life, it is necessary first of all that life not be evil and meaningless, and then one must have the power of reason to understand it. I realized why I had been wandering around such an obvious truth for so long and that in order to think and speak about the life of humankind, one must speak and think about the life of humankind and not about the life of a few parasites. This truth has always been the truth, like $2 \times 2 = 4$, but I had not acknowledged it, for in acknowledging that $2 \times 2 = 4$, I would have had to admit that I was not a good man. And it was more important and more pressing for me to feel that I was a good man than to admit that $2 \times 2 = 4$. But I came to love good people and to hate myself, and I acknowledged the truth. Now it all became clear to me.

Consider an executioner who has spent his life in torture and chopping off heads or a hopeless drunk or a madman who has wasted away in a dark room, who has despised this room and yet imagines that he would perish if he should leave it—what if these men should ask themselves, "What is life?" Clearly, they would be able to come up with only one answer, that life is the greatest of evils; and the madman's answer would be quite correct but only for him. What if I were such a madman? What if all of us who are wealthy and learned are such madmen?

And I realized that we were in fact such madmen. I, at any rate, was such a madman. To be sure, it is the nature of a bird to fly, gather food, build a nest; and when I see a bird doing this I rejoice in its joy. It is the nature of the goat, the hare, the wolf to feed, multiply, and nourish their young; and when they do this

I am firmly convinced that they are happy and that their lives are reasonable. What then should man do? He should earn his life in exactly the same way the animals do but with this one difference: that he will perish if he does it alone—he must live his life not for himself but for all. And when he does this, I am firmly convinced that he is happy and his life is reasonable. What, indeed, had I done in all my thirty years of conscious life? Not only had I failed to live my life for the sake of all, but I had not even lived it for myself. I had lived as a parasite, and once I had asked myself why I lived, the answer I received was: for nothing. If the meaning of human life lies in the way it is lived, then how could I, who had spent thirty years not living life but ruining it for myself and others, receive any reply other than this, that my life was meaningless and evil? It was indeed meaningless and evil.

The life of the world unfolds according to someone's will; the life of the world and our own lives are entrusted to someone's care. If we are to have any hope of understanding this will, then we must first of all fulfill it; we must do what is asked of us. And if I will not do what is asked of me, then I will never understand what is asked of me, much less what is asked of all of us and of the whole world.

If a naked, hungry beggar should be taken from the crossroads and led into an enclosed area in a magnificent establishment to be given food and drink, and if he should then be made to move some kind of lever up and down, it is obvious that before determining why he was brought there to move the lever and whether the structure of the establishment was reasonable, the beggar must first work the lever. If he will work it, then he will see that it operates a pump, that the pump draws up water, and that the water flows into a garden. Then he will be taken from the enclosed area and set to another task, and then he will gather fruits and enter into the joy of his lord. As he rises from lower to higher concerns, understanding more and more about the structure of the establishment and becoming part of it, he will never think to ask why he is there, and there is no way he will ever come to reproach his master.

Thus the simple, uneducated working people, whom we look upon as animals, do the will of their master without ever reproaching him. But we, the wise, consume everything the master provides without doing what he asks of us; instead, we sit in a circle and speculate on why we should do something so stupid as moving this lever up and down. And we have hit upon an answer. We have figured it out that either the master is stupid or he does not exist, while we alone are wise; only we feel that we are good for nothing and that we must somehow get rid of ourselves.

XII

Recognizing the errors of rational knowledge helped me to free myself from the temptations of idle reflection. The conviction that a knowledge of the truth can be found only in life led me to doubt that my own life was as it should be; and the one thing that saved me was that I was able to tear myself from my isolation, look at the true life of the simple working people, and realize that this alone is the true life. I realized that if I wanted to understand life and its meaning, I would have to live not the life of a parasite but the genuine life; and once I have accepted the meaning that is given to life by the real humanity that makes up life, I would have to test it out.

This is what happened to me at the time: in the course of a whole year, when almost every minute I was asking myself whether I should end it all with a rope or a bullet, when I was occupied with the thoughts and observations I have described, my heart was tormented with an agonizing feeling. This feeling I can only describe as a search for God.

I say that this search for God was born not of reason but of an emotion because it was a search that arose not from my thought process—indeed, it was in direct opposition to my thinking—but from my heart. It was a feeling of dread, of loneliness, of forlornness in the midst of all that was alien to me; and it was a feeling of hope for someone's help.

In spite of the fact that I was convinced of the impossibility of proving the existence of God (Kant* had shown me, and I had fully understood him, that there can be no such proof), I nonetheless searched for God in the hope that I might find him, and according to an old habit of prayer, I addressed the one for whom I searched and could not find. In my mind I would go over the conclusions of Kant and Schopenhauer regarding the impossibility of proving the existence of God, and I would try to refute them. Causation, I would say to myself, is not in the same category of thought as space and time. If I exist, then there is something that causes me to exist, the cause of all causes. And this cause of all that exists is called God; and I dwelled on this thought and tried with all my being to recognize the presence of this cause. As soon as I was conscious of the existence of such a power over me, I felt the possibility of life. But I asked myself, "What is this cause, this power? How am I to think about it? What is my relation to this thing I call God?" And only the answer that was familiar to me came into my head: "He is the creator, the provider of all things." I was not satisfied with this answer, and I felt that the thing I needed in order to live was still missing. I was overcome with

*Immanuel Kant (1724–1804) was a German philosopher whose critiques of reason raised questions concerning the possibility of knowledge and the foundations for the judgments we make about the world.

horror, and I began to pray to the one whom I sought, that he might help me. And the more I prayed, the more clear it became to me that he did not hear me and that there was absolutely no one I could turn to. My heart full of despair over the fact that there is no God, I cried, "Lord, have mercy on me, save me! O Lord, my God, show me the way!" But no one had mercy on me, and I felt that my life had come to a stop.

But again and again and from various directions I kept coming back to the conviction that I could not have come into the world without any motive, cause, or meaning, that I could not be the fledgling fallen from a nest that I felt myself to be. If I lie on my back in the tall grass and cry out like a fallen fledgling, it is because my mother brought me into the world, kept me warm, fed me, and loved me. But where is my mother now? If I have been cast out, then who has cast me out? I cannot help but feel that someone who loved me gave birth to me. Who is this someone? Again, God.

"He sees and knows of my search, my despair, my struggle," I would say to myself. "He exists." And as soon as I acknowledged this for an instant, life immediately rose up within me, and I could sense the possibility and even the joy of being. But again I would shift from the acknowledgment of the existence of God to a consideration of my relation to him, and again there arose before me the God who is our creator, the God of the Trinity, who sent his son, our Redeemer. And again, isolated from me and from the world, God would melt away before my eyes like a piece of ice; again nothing remained, again the source of life withered away. I was overcome with despair and felt that there was nothing for me to do but kill myself. And, worst of all, I felt that I could not bring myself to go through with it.

I slipped into these situations not two or three times but tens and hundreds of times—now joy and vitality, now despair and a consciousness of the impossibility of life.

I remember one day in early spring when I was alone in the forest listening to the sounds of the woods. I listened and thought about the one thing that had constantly occupied me for the last three years. Again I was searching for God.

"Very well," I said to myself. "So there is no God like the one I have imagined; the only reality is my life. There is no such God. And nothing, no miracle of any kind, can prove there is, because miracles exist only in my irrational imagination."

"But where does my notion of God, of the one whom I seek, come from?" I asked myself. And again with this thought there arose in me joyous waves of life. Everything around me came to life, full of meaning. But my joy did not last long. My mind continued its work. "The concept of God," I told myself, "is not God. A concept is something that occurs within me; the concept of God is something I can conjure up inside myself at will. This is not what I seek. I am seeking that without which there could be no life." Once again everything within me and around me began to die; again I felt the longing to kill myself.

But at that point I took a closer look at myself and at what had been happening within me; and I remembered the hundreds of times I had gone through these deaths and revivals. I remembered that I had lived only when I believed in God. Then, as now, I said to myself, "As long as I know God, I live; when I forget, when I do not believe in him, I die." What are these deaths and revivals? It is clear that I do not live whenever I lose my faith in the existence of God, and I would have killed myself long ago if I did not have some vague hope of finding God. I truly live only whenever I am conscious of him and seek him. "What, then, do I seek?" a voice cried out within me. "He is there, the one without whom there could be no life." To know God and to live come to one and the same thing. God is life.

"Live, seeking God, for there can be no life without God."
And more powerfully than ever a light shone within me and all
around me, and this light has not abandoned me since.

Thus I was saved from suicide. When and how this transformation within me was accomplished, I could not say. Just as the
life force within me was gradually and imperceptibly destroyed,
and I encountered the impossibility of life, the halting of life, and
the need to murder myself, so too did this life force return to me
gradually and imperceptibly. And the strange thing is that the life
force which returned to me was not new but very old; it was the
same force that had guided me during the early periods of my life.
In essence I returned to the first things, to the things of childhood
and youth. I returned to a faith in that will which gave birth to
me and which asked something of me; I returned to the conviction
that the single most important purpose in my life was to be better,
to live according to this will. I returned to the conviction that I
could find the expression of this will in something long hidden
from me, something that all of humanity had worked out for its
own guidance; in short, I returned to a belief in God, in moral
perfection, and in a tradition that instills life with meaning. The
only difference was that I had once accepted all this on an unconscious level, while now I knew that I could not live without it.

What happened to me was something like the following.
Unable to recall how I got there, I found myself in a boat that had
been launched from some unknown shore; the way to the other
shore was pointed out to me, the oars were placed in my inexperienced hands, and I was left alone. I worked the oars as best
I knew how and rowed on. But the further I paddled toward the
center, the faster became the current that took me off-course, and
I encountered more and more people who, like myself, were being
carried away by the current. There were a few who continued to
row; some had thrown away their oars. There were large boats,

does it take deep despair to find faith

enormous ships, filled with people; some struggled against the current, others gave themselves up to it. And, looking downstream at everyone being carried along by the current, the further I rowed, the more I forgot the way that had been pointed out to me. At the very center of the current, in the throng of boats and ships being carried downstream, I lost my way altogether and threw down my oars. All around me, in joy and triumph, people rushed downstream under sail and oar, assuring me and each other that there could be no other direction. And I believed them and moved along with them. And I was carried off a long way, so far that I heard the roar of the rapids in which I was bound to perish and saw boats being destroyed in them. Then I came to my senses. For a long time I could not understand what had happened to me. I saw before me the singular ruin toward which I was rushing headlong and which I feared, I could not see salvation anywhere, and I did not know what to do. But, looking back, I saw countless boats that were relentlessly struggling against the current, and I remembered the oars and the way to the shore and began to pull against the current and head back upstream toward it.

The shore was God, the stream was tradition, and the oars were the free will given to me to make it to the shore where I would be joined with God. Thus the force of life was renewed within me, and I began to live once again.

XIII

I renounced the life of our class and recognized that this is not life but only the semblance of life, that the conditions of luxury under which we live make it impossible for us to understand life, and that in order to understand life I must understand not the life of those of us who are parasites but the life of the simple working people, those who create life and give it meaning. The simple working people all around me were the Russian people, and I turned to them and to the meaning they gave life. This meaning, if it is possible to express it, was the following. Every human being has been brought into the world according to the will of God. And God created us in such a way that every human being can either save his own soul or destroy it. Man's task in life is to save his soul. In order to save our souls, we must live according to the ways of God, and in order to live according to the ways of God, we must renounce the sensual pleasures of life; we must labor, suffer, and be kind and humble. This is the meaning that the people have derived from all the religious teachings handed down and conferred upon them by their pastors, and from the tradition that lives in them, expressed through their legends, sayings, and stories. This meaning was clear to me and dear to my heart. But along with the meaning rooted in the faith of the people there was much that repelled me and seemed inexplicable to me, much that was inextricably bound to the non-Raskolnik people among whom I lived: the sacraments, church services, fasts, bowing before relics and icons. The people could not separate one thing from another, and nor could I. Despite the fact that much of what came out of the faith of the people was strange to me, I accepted all of it, attended services, participated in the morning and evening prayers, fasted and prepared for communion; and for the first time there was nothing in opposition to my reason. The very thing that had initially seemed impossible to me now excited no opposition within me.

My relation to faith at that time was quite different from what it was now. At first life itself seemed to be full of meaning, and I regarded faith as an arbitrary confirmation of a certain position that was quite unnecessary to me, irrational, and unconnected to life. At that time I asked myself what meaning such a position could have, and once I was convinced it had no meaning I cast it aside. Now, however, I was certain that my life did not have and could not have any meaning, and not only did the principles of faith no longer seem unnecessary to me, but experience had unquestionably led me to the conviction that only the principles of faith gave life meaning. At first I looked upon them as useless gibberish, but now I knew that even though I might not understand them, there was meaning in them, and I told myself that I must learn to understand them.

My reasoning proceeded in the following manner. "Like man and his power of reason," I said to myself, "the knowledge of faith arises from a mysterious origin. This origin is God, the source of the human mind and body. Just as God has bestowed my body upon me a bit at a time, so has he imparted to me my reason and understanding of life; thus the stages in the development of this understanding cannot be false. Everything that people truly believe must be true; it may be expressed in differing ways, but it cannot be a lie. Therefore, if I take it to be a lie, this merely indicates that I have failed to understand it." And then I said to myself, "The essence of any faith lies in giving life a meaning that cannot be destroyed by death. Naturally, if faith is to answer the questions of a tsar dying in the midst of luxury, an old slave tormented in his labor, an ignorant child, an aged sage, a half-witted old lady, a happy young woman, and a youth consumed by passions; if it is to answer the questions asked by people living under radically different circumstances of life and education; if there is but a single response to the one eternal question in life of why I live and what will become of my life, then this answer, though essentially everywhere the same, will be manifested in an infinite variety of ways. And the more unique, true, and profound this answer is, then, of course, the more strange and outrageous will seem the attempts to express it, depending on the upbringing and position of each individual." But even though I thought these ruminations justified the peculiarities of the ritualistic aspect of faith, they were not sufficient for me to perform acts that seemed dubious to me, especially when it came to the faith that had become the single concern of my life. With all my soul I longed to be in a position to join with the people in performing the rites of their faith, but I could not do it. I felt that I would be lying to myself, mocking what was sacred to me, if I were to go through with it. But here our new Russian theological works came to my aid.

According to the explanation provided by these theologians, the fundamental dogma of faith is rooted in the infallibility of the Church. The truth of everything the Church stands for follows from this dogma as a necessary conclusion. As an assembly of believers who are united in love and who therefore possess true knowledge, the Church became the basis for my faith. I told myself that it is not for any one man to attain divine truth; it is revealed only through a union of all people joined together by love. If the truth is to be found, there must be no division; and if there is to be no division, we must love and be reconciled with those who do not agree with us. Truth is a revelation of love, and therefore if you do not submit to the rituals of the Church, you destroy love; and if you destroy love, you lose all possibility of knowing truth. At the time I did not recognize the sophistry that lay in this line of reasoning. I failed to see that a union in love may result in the greatest love but cannot reveal divine truth as expressed in the definitive words of the Nicene Creed; I failed to see that love cannot make a given expression of truth binding on a union of believers. At the time I did not realize the error in this line of thought, and thanks to it I found it possible to accept and perform all the rites of the Orthodox Church without understanding a large part of them. I struggled with all my soul to avoid all discussions, all contradictions, and tried to explain as reasonably as possible the doctrines of the Church with which I was in conflict.

In carrying out the rituals of the Church I restrained my reason and submitted myself to the tradition adopted by all of humanity. I joined with my ancestors and loved ones, with my father, mother, and grandparents. They and all before them believed and lived and brought me into the world. I joined with all the millions who made up the people whom I respected. Nor was there anything wrong with these acts in themselves (the indulgence of lusts was what I considered wrong). When I rose early in the morning to go to the church service I knew I was doing something good, if only because I was sacrificing my physical comfort to humble the pride of my intellect, to be closer to my ancestors and contemporaries, to seek the meaning of life. It was the same with the preparation for communion, the daily reading of prayers and the gestures that go with it, and even the observance of all the fasts. No matter how insignificant these sacrifices were, they were made in the name of something good. I prepared for communion, fasted, and observed the hours of prayer both at home and in church. When listening to the church services I tried to grasp every word and give it meaning whenever I could. At mass the most important words for me were "Let us love one another in unity." But I disregarded the words that followed—"We believe in the Father, the Son, and the Holy Ghost"—because I could not understand them.

XIV

At the time I found it so necessary to believe in order to live that I unconsciously hid from myself the contradictions and the obscurities in the religious teachings. There was, however, a limit to this interpretation of the rituals. Although the most important words in the liturgy became more and more clear to me; although I somehow explained to myself the words "Remembering our Sovereign Lady, Holy Mother of God, and all the saints, let us one and all devote the whole of our lives to Christ, God"; although I explained the frequent repetition of prayers for the tsar and his family by the fact that they were more subject to temptation than others and were therefore in greater need of the prayers; although I explained the prayers for the vanquishing of our enemies by saying that the enemy was evil, these prayers and other things, such as the hymn of the cherubim, the mystery of the bread and wine, the adoration of the Virgin and so on, nearly two-thirds of the service either had no meaning at all or made me feel like I was lying when I tried to explain them, which would mean I was destroying my relation to God and would lose all possibility of faith.

I felt the same way when celebrating the main holidays. I could understand the observance of the sabbath—that is, the consecration of one day in the week for communion with God. But the most important holiday was in remembrance of the Resurrection, the reality of which I could neither imagine nor comprehend. And the weekly holiday, Sunday, was named for this Resurrection.* On this day the mystery of the Eucharist was observed, which was utterly incomprehensible to me. With the exception of Christmas, the other twelve holidays were in remembrance of miracles, which I tried not to think about in order to avoid denying them: the Ascension, the Pentecost, the Epiphany, the Intercession of the Virgin, and so on. As I celebrated these holidays, feeling that the greatest importance was being attached to what I considered least important, I either invented an explanation that

*The Russian word for "Sunday," *voskresen'e,* is taken from the word for "resurrection," *voskresenie.*

appeased me or I closed my eyes so I would not see the thing seducing me.

All this struck me most powerfully when I took part in the most common and what are regarded as the most important of the sacraments: baptism and communion. Here I was in conflict with nothing incomprehensible but with matters that were quite easy to understand; it seemed to me that these acts were deceptive in nature, and I was caught in a dilemma—I had either to reject them or lie about them.

I shall never forget the agonizing feeling that went through me when I took communion for the first time in many years. The service, the confession, the collects—all of it was understandable to me and excited in me the joyous realization that the meaning of life was being revealed to me. I explained the communion to myself as an act performed in remembrance of Christ, signifying the cleansing of sin and the complete acceptance of Christ's teachings. If this explanation was rather artificial, I took no notice of its being so. As I humbled and surrendered myself to the confessor, a simple and timid priest, it was such a joy for me to lay bare all the filth in my soul, repenting of my sins; it was such a joy to be united in thought with the strivings of the fathers who had composed the prayers of the collects; it was such a joy to be joined with the faithful and the believers that I had no sense of the artificial nature of my explanation. But when I neared the gates of the kingdom, and the priest asked me to repeat what I believed and that what I was about to swallow was actually flesh and blood, it cut me to the heart; this was a small but false note, a cruel demand placed on someone who obviously had never had any idea of what faith was.

Although now I allow myself to deem it a cruel demand, at the time I had no notion that it was; it simply caused me unspeakable pain. I no longer took up the position I had adopted in my youth, supposing that everything in life was clear. Indeed, I had come to faith because apart from it I could find nothing but ruin, and therefore I could not cast faith away; so I submitted. In my soul I discovered a feeling that helped me to endure this. It was a feeling of self-abasement and humility. I humbled myself and swallowed the flesh and the blood without any blasphemous emotions, and with a longing to believe, but the blow had already left its mark. Knowing beforehand what awaited me, I could not go through with it a second time.

Nevertheless I continued to perform the church rituals, and I still believed that there was truth in the doctrine I adhered to; and then something happened that is clear to me now but at the time seemed odd.

I was listening to an illiterate peasant, a pilgrim, talking about God, faith, life, and salvation, and a knowledge of faith was opened up to me. I grew closer to the people as I listened to their reflections on life and faith, and I began to understand the truth more and more. The same thing happened to me when I read the Martyrology and the Prologues;* they became my favorite reading. Taking exception to the miracles and viewing them as fables that expressed an idea, these readings revealed to me the meaning of life. Among them were the lives of Macarius the Great† and Prince Ioasaph (the story of the Buddha), the writings of John Chrysostom,‡ the story of the traveler in the well, of the monk who discovered gold and of Peter the Publican; they included the

*The Martyrology and the Prologues contain tales and legends of the saints and their sufferings.
†Better known as Macarius the Egyptian, Macarius the Great was a fourth-century saint and hermit renowned for his miracles and his wisdom.
‡John Chrysostom (1594–1646) was a Franciscan spiritual leader and writer from France.

histories of the martyrs, all of whom proclaimed that life does not end with death. These were tales of illiterate, stupid men who found salvation though they knew nothing of the teachings of the Church.

But as soon as I mixed with learned believers or picked up their books, a certain doubt, dissatisfaction, and bitterness over their arguments rose up within me, and I felt that the more I grasped their discourses, the further I strayed from the truth and the closer I came to the abyss.

XV

Many times I have envied the peasants for their illiteracy and their lack of education. They could see nothing false in those tenets of faith which to me seemed to have arisen from patent nonsense; they could accept them and believe in the truth, the same truth I believed in. But unhappily for me, it was clear that the truth was tied to a lie with the finest of threads and that I could not accept it in such a form.

Thus I lived for about three years, and when, like one possessed, I started to inch my way toward the truth, led only by instinct toward the place where the light seemed to shine, seeming untruths did not bother me so much. When I failed to understand something, I would say to myself, "I am guilty, I am wrong." But the more I came to be filled with the truths I studied, the more they became the foundation of life, until untruths became increasingly difficult and disturbing. The line separating the things I did not know how to understand from those I could understand only by lying to myself became more distinct.

In spite of doubts and torments, I was still clinging to the

Orthodox Church. But questions of life that had to be resolved kept coming up, and the Church's resolution of these questions was in direct opposition to the faith by which I lived; this is what finally led me to renounce the possibility of a relationship with the Orthodox Church. These questions, first of all, pertained to the relation between the Orthodox Church and other churches, its relation to Catholicism and the so-called Raskolniks. As a result of my interest in faith at the time, I became acquainted with believers of various creeds: Catholics, Protestants, Old Believers, Molokans,* and others. And I met many people among them of the highest moral character who were truly believers. I wanted to be a brother to these people. But what happened? The doctrine that had promised me a union with all through love and a single faith was the very doctrine that, in the mouths of its finest adherents, told me that all these people were living in a lie, that the thing that gave them the strength to live was a temptation of the devil, and that we alone are in possession of the only truth possible. And I saw that the members of the Orthodox Church regarded as heretics everyone who did not profess the same beliefs as they, just as the Catholics and others viewed the members of the Orthodox Church as heretics; I saw that although she tried to hide it, the Orthodox Church regarded as enemies everyone who did not adopt the same outward symbols and expressions of faith as she. And it had to be this way because, first of all, the assertion that you live in a lie while I live in the truth is the most cruel thing one person can say to another, and, secondly, because a man who loves his children and his brothers cannot but regard as enemies those who want to convert his children and his brothers to a false

*The Molokans, or "milk drinkers," made up a sect that did not believe in fasting, scorned the ceremonial aspects of religion, and used the Bible as the sole foundation for their practices and beliefs.

faith. And this enmity grows in proportion to one's knowledge of the teachings of doctrine. Even I, who had supposed that the truth lay in a union of love, was forced to recognize that the teachings of doctrine destroy the very thing they set out to produce.

The temptation is obvious to educated people like ourselves who live in countries where a variety of creeds are professed and who see the contemptuous, self-righteous, unflinching disdain the Catholic has for the Orthodox and the Protestant, the Orthodox for the Catholic and the Protestant, and the Protestant for both; this also applies to the Old Believers, the Revivalists, the Shakers,* and all the rest. It is so evident that at first glance it is quite puzzling. You say to yourself, "It cannot be as simple as all that. Is it possible for people to fail to see that even though two positions are in conflict with each other, neither one may harbor the single truth that should constitute the basis for faith? There must be some kind of explanation here." I too thought there was some kind of explanation, and I looked for it and read everything I could on the subject and consulted everyone I knew. But the only explanation I could find was the one according to which the Sumsky hussars regard themselves as the finest regiment in the world, while the yellow Uhlans considered themselves to be the best in the world. Clergymen of all denominations, the finest representatives of their creeds, all told me the same thing—namely, that theirs was the true belief and all the others were erroneous, and that the only thing they could do for the others was to pray for them. I visited archimandrites, bishops, elder monks, and ascetic monks, none of whom made any attempt to explain this pitfall to me. Only one interpreted the matter for me, but his explanation was such that I asked no more questions of anyone.

*The Shakers, members of a millenarian sect originating in England in 1747, practiced celibacy and an ascetic communal life.

I have said that for any unbelievers returning to faith (and here I have in mind our entire younger generation), the first question to be posed is: why does the truth lie not in the Lutheran or in the Catholic Church but in the Orthodox Church? One is taught in high school and cannot help but know what the peasant does not know—namely, that the Protestants and the Catholics make exactly the same claim to the one and only truth that our own faith does. Historical proofs perverted by each creed to suit its own purpose are insufficient. Is it not possible, as I have suggested, that in attaining a higher level of understanding the differences would disappear, just as they do for those who are genuine believers? Is it not possible to go further down the path along which we have set out with the Old Believers? They have claimed that there is an alternative to the way in which we make the sign of the cross, shouting hallelujahs and moving about the altar. It has been said, "You believe in the Nicene Creed and in the seven sacraments, and so do we. Let us keep to that; as for the rest of it, you may do as you please. Thus we may be united by placing the essential elements of faith higher than the nonessential." Is it not possible to say to the Catholics, "You believe in this and that, in what is important; as far as the *filioque** and the Pope are concerned, do as you please?" Is it not possible to say the same thing to the Protestants and join together in the one thing needful? I said this to one person who agreed with my thinking, but he told me that such concessions would arouse the censure of the clergy, who would object that this marks a departure from the faith of our forefathers and brings about dissent, and that it is

*Filioque, meaning "and from the Son," is a word that was added to the Nicene-Constantinopolitan Creed in the Latin Church. It followed the phrase "the Holy Spirit . . . who proceeds from the Father," suggesting that the Holy Spirit arises both from the Father and from the Son.

incumbent upon the clergy to preserve in all things the purity of the Greco-Russian Orthodox faith handed down to the Church by our ancestors.

Then I understood it all. I am searching for faith, for the force of life, but they seek the best means for fulfilling what people consider to be certain human obligations. And in meeting these human duties they perform them in an all-too-human fashion. No matter what they may say about their compassion for their brothers who have gone astray or about their prayers for those who will come before the judgment seat of the Most High, human duties can only be carried out by force; and force has always been implemented, is now being implemented, and always will be implemented. If each of two religions believes that it alone abides in the truth while the other lives in a lie, then since they want to lead their brothers to the truth, they will go on preaching their own doctrine. And if a false doctrine is preached to the inexperienced children of the Church that dwells in the truth, then that Church cannot help but burn books and banish a person who is leading her children into temptation. What is to be done with a sectary who passionately proclaims what the Church regards as a false faith and who is leading the children of the Church astray in the most important thing in life, in faith? What is to be done with him except to chop off his head or lock him up? In the time of Alexis Mikhailovich* they were burned at the stake, that is, they met with the full measure of the law; the same is true in our own times: they are locked up in solitary confinement. When I turned my attention to what is done in the name of religion I was horrified and very nearly withdrew from the Orthodox Church entirely. Another thing was the Church's relation to questions of life with

*Alexis Mikhailovich (1629–1676) was the second Romanov tsar of Russia (1645–76) and the father of Peter the Great.

respect to its attitude toward war and executions.

During this time Russia was at war.* And in the name of Christian love Russians were killing their brothers. There was no way to avoid thinking about this. There was no way to ignore the fact that murder was evil and contrary to the most fundamental tenets of any faith. Nonetheless, in the churches they were praying for the success of our weapons, and the teachers of faith looked upon this murder as the outcome of faith. And not only was the murder that came with the war sanctioned, but during the disturbances that followed the war I saw members of the Church, its teachers, monks, and ascetics, condoning the murder of straying, helpless youths. I turned my attention to everything that was done by people who claimed to be Christians, I was horrified.

XVI

I no longer had any doubts and was firmly convinced that the teachings of the faith with which I had associated myself were not all true. At one time I would have said that all of it was a lie; but now it was impossible to say this. There could be no doubt that all of the people had a knowledge of the truth, for otherwise they would not be living. Moreover, this knowledge of the truth was already accessible to me; already I was living by it and could feel that this was indeed the truth; but in these teachings there was also a lie. There was no doubt about it. And everything that had previously repelled me was now vividly before me. Although I could see that among the people there was less tinged with the lie

*Here Tolstoy is referring to the Russo-Turkish War of 1877–78, which ended when Russia advanced on Istanbul. This was also a time when Russia was plagued by terrorism.

that repelled me than among the representatives of the Church, I could still see that even among the people the lie was mixed with the truth.

But where did the lie come from and where the truth? Both the lie and the truth came from what was known as the Church. Both the lie and the truth were part of a tradition, part of a so-called sacred tradition, part of the Scriptures.

And, like it or not, I came to study and analyze the Scriptures and the tradition; I undertook an analysis that up till now I had feared to undertake.

Thus I turned to a study of the very theology that at one time I had contemptuously rejected as unnecessary. Then it had struck me as so much useless nonsense; then I had been surrounded by life's phenomena, which I thought to be clear and full of meaning. Now I would have been glad to free myself of everything that did not foster a healthy mind, but I did not know how to escape. Rooted in this religious teaching, or at least directly connected to it, is the one meaning of life that has been revealed to me. No matter how outrageous it might seem to me in my old stubborn intellect, here lies the one hope of salvation. It must be examined carefully and attentively in order to be understood, even if I do not understand it in the way I understand the position of science. I do not and cannot seek such an understanding of it due to the peculiar nature of the knowledge of faith. I shall not seek an explanation of all things. I know that the explanation of all things, like the origin of all things, must remain hidden in infinity. But I do want to understand in order that I might be brought to the inevitably incomprehensible; I want all that is incomprehensible to be such not because the demands of the intellect are not sound (they are sound, and apart from them I understand nothing) but because I perceive the limits of the intellect. I want to understand, so that any instance of the incomprehensible occurs as a necessity of reason and not as an obligation to believe.

I have no doubt that there is truth in the doctrine; but there can also be no doubt that it harbors a lie; and I must find the truth and the lie so I can tell them apart. This is what I set out to do. What I found that was a lie, what I found that was the truth, and the conclusions I came to are presented in the subsequent portion of this work, which, if someone should find it useful, will probably be published someday, somewhere.*

———————

I wrote the above three years ago.†

The other day, as I was looking over this printed portion and returning to the thoughts and feelings that went through me when I was experiencing all this, I had a dream. This dream expressed for me in a condensed form everything I lived through and wrote about; therefore I think that for those who have understood me, a description of the dream will refresh, clarify, and gather into one piece what has been discussed at length in these pages. Here is the dream: I see that I am lying in bed. Feeling neither good nor bad, I am lying on my back. But I begin to wonder whether it is a good thing for me to be lying there; and it seems to me that there is something wrong with my legs; whether they are too short or uneven, I do not know, but there is something awkward about them. As I start to move my legs, I begin to wonder how and on what I am lying, something that up till now had not entered my mind. Looking about my bed, I see that I am lying on some cords

*The work Tolstoy is referring to is *An Investigation of Dogmatic Theology*, which he never published.
†This last portion of the *Confession* was written in 1882.

91

woven together and attached to the sides of the bed. My heels are resting on one of the cords and my lower legs on another in an uncomfortable way. Somehow I know that these cords can be shifted. Moving one leg, I push away the furthest cord. It seems to me that it will be more comfortable that way. But I have pushed it too far away; I try to catch it, but this movement causes another cord to slip out from under my legs, leaving them hanging down. I rearrange my whole body, quite certain I will be settled now; but this movement causes still other cords to shift and slip out from under me, and I see that the whole situation is getting worse: the whole lower part of my body is sinking and hanging down, and my feet are not touching the ground. I am supported only along the upper part of my back, and for some reason I begin to feel not only uncomfortable but terrified. Only now do I ask myself what had not yet occurred to me: where am I and what am I lying on? I begin to look around, and the first place I look is down toward where my body is dangling, in the direction where I feel I must soon fall. I look below, and I cannot believe my eyes. I am resting on a height such as I could never have imagined, a height altogether unlike that of the highest tower or mountain.

I cannot even tell whether I can see anything down below in the bottomless depths of the abyss over which I am hanging and into which I am drawn. My heart stops, and I am overcome with horror. It is horrible to look down there. I feel that if I look down, I will immediately slip from the last cord and perish. I do not look, yet not looking is worse, for now I am thinking about what will happen to me as soon as the last cord breaks. I feel that I am losing the last ounce of my strength from sheer terror and that my back is slowly sinking lower and lower. Another instant and I shall break away. And then a thought occurs to me: this cannot be real. It is just a dream. I will wake up. I try to wake up, but I cannot. "What am I to do, what am I to do?" I ask myself, looking up. Above me there is also an abyss. I gaze into this abyss of sky and try to forget about the one below, and I actually do forget. The infinity below repels and horrifies me; the infinity above attracts me and gives me strength. Thus I am hanging over the abyss suspended by the last of the cords that have not yet slipped out from under me. I know I am hanging there, but I am only looking upward, and my terror passes. As it happens in a dream, a voice is saying, "Mark this, this is it!" I gaze deeper and deeper into the infinity above me, and I seem to grow calm. I recall everything that has happened, and I remember how it all came about: how I moved my legs, how I was dangling there, the horror that came over me, and how I was saved from the horror by looking up. And I ask myself, "Well, am I still hanging here?" And as soon as I glance around, I feel with my whole body a support that is holding me up. I can see that I am no longer dangling or falling but am firmly supported. I ask myself how I am being supported; I touch myself, look around, and see that there is a single cord underneath the center of my body, that when I look up I am lying on it firmly balanced, and that it alone has supported me all along. As it happens in a dream, the mechanism by which I am supported seems quite natural, understandable, and beyond doubt, in spite of the fact that when I am awake the mechanism is completely incomprehensible. In my sleep I am even astonished that I had not understood this before. It seems that there is a pillar beside me and that there is no doubt of the solidity of the pillar, even though it has nothing to stand on. The cord is somehow very cleverly yet very simply attached to the pillar, leading out from it, and if you place the middle of your body on the cord and look up, there cannot even be a question of falling. All this was clear to me, and I was glad and at peace. Then it is as if someone is saying to me, "See that you remember." And I awoke.

SELECTED BIBLIOGRAPHY

Bayley, John. *Tolstoy and the Novel.* New York: Viking, 1967.

Blagoy, D. D. *Tvorchestvo L. N. Tolstogo.* Moscow, 1959.

Bychkov, S. D. *L. N. Tolstoy v russkoi kritike.* 3rd ed. Moscow, 1960.

Christian, Reginald F. *Tolstoy: A Critical Introduction.* London: Cambridge University Press, 1969.

Crankshaw, Edward. *Tolstoy.* New York: Viking, 1974.

Eikhenbaum, B. M. *Lev Tolstoy.* Munich: Wilhelm Fink, 1968.

———. *Lev Tolstoy: Semidesyatye gody.* Leningrad, 1974.

Fausset, Hugh I'Anson. *Tolstoy: The Inner Drama.* London: Jonathan Cape, 1927.

Flew, Anthony. "Tolstoi and the Meaning of Life." *Ethics* 73 (1963): 110–18.

Fueloep-Miller, René. "Tolstoy the Apostolic Crusader." *Russian Review* 19 (1960): 99–121.

Greenwood, E. B. *Tolstoy: The Comprehensive Vision.* New York: St. Martin's Press, 1975.

Gusev, N. N. *Lev Nikolaevich Tolstoy.* Moscow, 1963.

Matlaw, Ralph, ed. *Tolstoy: A Collection of Critical Essays.* Englewood Cliffs, NJ: Prentice-Hall, 1967.

Maude, Aylmer. *The Life of Tolstoy.* 5th ed. New York: Dodd, Mead and Co., 1911.

Merezhkovsky, Dmitri. *Tolstoi as Man and Artist.* Authorized English trans. New York: G. P. Putnam's Sons, 1902.

Shklovsky, V. *Lev Tolstoy.* 2nd ed. Moscow, 1967.

Simmons, Ernest J. *Leo Tolstoy.* Boston: Little, Brown and Co., 1946.

———. *Tolstoy.* London: Routledge & Kegan Paul, 1973.

Spence, G. W. *Tolstoy the Ascetic.* New York: Barnes & Noble, 1967.

Steiner, George. *Tolstoy or Dostoevsky.* New York: Alfred Knopf, 1959.

Tolstaya, S. A. *The Diary of Tolstoy's Wife: 1860–1891.* Trans. by Alexander Werth. New York: Payson & Clarke, 1928.

Troyat, Henri. *Tolstoi.* Paris: Fayard, 1965.

Zhdanov, V. A. *Ot "Anny Kareninoi" k "Voskreseniyu."* Moscow, 1968.